LOCKE'S DISTILLERY

LOCKE'S DISTILLERY

*

A History

ANDREW BIELENBERG

ESTABLISHED 1757.
THE OLDEST DISTILLERY IN IRELAND.

John Locke & Co. Ltd.
Distillers of Pure Pot Still Whiskey.

THE LILLIPUT PRESS

First published 1993 by
THE LILLIPUT PRESS
62–63 Sitric Road, Arbour Hill
Dublin 7, Ireland
www.lilliputpress.ie
Reissued 2007

ISBN 978 1 874675 04 4 hbk
978 1 874675 05 1 pbk

A CIP record for this title
is available from The British Library.

Set in 11 pt on 13 pt Galliard by Mermaid Turbulence
Printed in England by MPG Books, Bodmin, Cornwall

CONTENTS

FOREWORD

When the first new whiskey flows out of the pot still in Kilbeggan in 2007 it will be the start of yet another chapter in the long and glorious history of the oldest licensed whiskey distillery in the world. There are usurpers for the title of 'oldest licensed distillery' but as Andrew Bielenberg, in his scholarly essay, 'The Irish distilling industry under the Union' (from *Refiguring Ireland*, 2003) points out below, there is no evidence to support their claims. The reissue of this book is timed to coincide with three significant events, the 250th anniversary of the establishment of a whiskey distillery on the site, the restart of whiskey distilling after a lapse of fifty years and the 20th anniversary of the start of Cooley Distillery, the owner of Kilbeggan distillery.

Few ventures survive for 250 years. The history of distilling in Kilbeggan shows numerous projects by different families and companies, but always Irish owned. The site has hosted breweries, pig farms and bonded warehouses between extended periods of whiskey distilling. Though the distillery is closely associated with the Locke family, who owned it for over a hundred years, the MacManus and Codd families ran operations in the late eighteenth century. Bacchus and his followers, looking down on Kilbeggan, must have believed that the Locke's liquidation in the late 1950s was the final straw. But a few devoted townspeople did not want the historic operation to disappear like every other Irish distillery except one, so they formed a committee to preserve the wonderful machinery and structure. In acquiring the assets of John Locke in 1988 we in Cooley saw the advantages of impressive granite warehouses and a fascinating museum, with the potential to relaunch famous old brands as well as to restart the oldest licensed distillery in the country.

In the years since, thousands of casks of whiskey have slumbered in peace, in conditions as perfect as you can get for maturing whiskey, and the sound of the cooper's hammer once again rings through the distillery. The ultimate purpose, however, in acquiring Kilbeggan was to restart distillation. This will happen in 2007 during the 250th celebrations.

The renaissance in Irish whiskey holds great promise for an Irish industry that once dominated the world. Whiskey is Irish, every other whiskey, no matter how good, is a mere copy. From a position of dominance in the late nineteenth century Irish whiskey sales fell in the 1970s to less than 2 per cent of world whisk(e)y consumption. The distilling industry in Ireland all but disappeared, becoming a foreign-owned monopoly, distilling only in two locations. The pot stills in Kilbeggan went cold in 1953. Now there is a revival.

Cooley Distillery and Kilbeggan play a critical role in this revival. Single malts of the highest quality, including the unique peated 'Connemara', and premium blends like the 'Kilbeggan', are matured in 200-year-old warehouses. The start-up of distilling, albeit on a small scale, is a further step towards reclaiming the rightful position of Kilbeggan in the world hierarchy of famous distilleries.

JOHN J. TEELING
March 2007

vi

INTRODUCTION

Although the Irish distilling industry has received some attention from historians, the definitive work on the subject has yet to be written. E.B. Maguire's *Irish Whiskey* is useful, most notably in regard to the evolution of the excise infrastructure and government intervention in the industry. Weir's work on the patent still producers and Scottish involvement in the Irish industry is important for the period between the mid-nineteenth century and the 1920s.[1] But the major lacuna in our knowledge of the history of distilling in Ireland can be filled only by more studies of individual distilleries. To date, Bushmills is the only distillery to have produced such a history.[2]

The only detailed regional study of the industry covers County Offaly.[3] Locke's, just across the border in County Westmeath, falls within the same constellation of midland distilleries. For centuries, excellent barley has been grown in the midlands, which attracted people with a knowledge of the art of distilling whiskey. (Barley accounts for the lion's share of the distiller's costs, even today.) Another advantage was a supply of cheap fuel, turf, which could be readily acquired in the extensive boglands of the region. Many distillers, including Locke's, switched to using coal with the advent of the canal era, since British coal could be imported via Dublin at reasonable costs. But at the end of the 1940s, Locke's reverted to using the local turf, since it had once again become cost-effective, and provided a more even heat to the stills.

Locke's was typical of many small distilleries operating in rural Ireland in the eighteenth and nineteenth centuries.

What makes Locke's unique is that it started earlier and lasted much longer; most small distilleries had gone out of business by the 1930s.

The surviving business records of the distilling industry mainly relate to the larger urban distilleries in Dublin, Belfast and Cork, which dominated the industry by the end of the nineteenth century. Very little remains from any of the small rural distilleries in the south of Ireland. Fortunately, Locke's is an exception in this respect; a certain number of company records have survived and are now kept in the National Library.[4] The buildings and industrial archaeology of these rural distilleries very rarely survive. But again, happily, Locke's is one of the exceptions to the rule; the machinery and buildings are now an important part of Ireland's industrial heritage. Both this and the extant archival material make Locke's the most important case-study of a small rural Irish pot still distillery.

Locke's can proudly contend to be the oldest distillery in Ireland, despite the claims by Bushmills, who would have us believe that they are the oldest distillery not only in Ireland, but in the world. They base their claim on a quote from *Erck's Repertory* which relates to a licence granted to Thomas Phillipps Kt. in 1608:

To sir Thomas Phillipps, Knt., and such his assignes, as shall be allowed by the chiefe governor of Ireland, was granted on the 20th of Apriell, in the sixt year, lisence, for the next seaven yeres, within the countie of Colerane, otherwise called O Cahanes countrey, or within the territorie called the Rowte, in co. Antrim, by himselfe or his servauntes, to make drawe, and distill such and soe great quantities of aquavite, usquabagh and aqua composita, as he or his assignes shall think fitt....[5]

On this evidence the author argues that a distillery was established in Bushmills in 1608, which is the predecessor to the existing one. But it cannot be assumed that because Phillipps was granted a licence to distil in the Rowte in 1608, he established a distillery in the same year, on the ground where the Bushmills distillery now stands. The Rowte (or the Route) covered a much greater area than the present-day site. The company historian, Alf McCreary, points out that for many years, 1784 was the date registered on all company literature and products. It is highly unlikely that the company would have used this date if the distillery had been established earlier than this. It therefore seems most probable that 1784 was the year when the existing distillery was founded.

There were four licensed distilleries operating in Bushmills in 1782 when the first surviving return of all the licensed distilleries in Ireland was published for the Irish parliament. There were also three operating in Kilbeggan at this time. As chapter 1 will show, there is strong evidence to suggest that one of these concerns was located on the site of the existing distillery.[6]

The common practice in 1608 was for the Crown to grant patents to individuals like Phillipps at an agreed price. This gave them a monopoly on the right to make whiskey in a particular area. During the period covered by this licence (usually seven years, as in the case of Phillipps) the patentee could allow others to distil spirits at whatever charge he was able to secure.[7] The Lord Deputy granted such licences to people all over Ireland; in 1617, for example, he granted one to 'Anthony Atkinson in Philipstowne, and other places in King's county, Eastmeath and Westmeath'.[8] In March 1608 (prior to Phillipps' licence being granted in April), the Lord Deputy issued similar licences to people in Galway, Munster and Leinster.[8] It is probable that whiskey was being made in Bushmills at this time, but there is nothing noteworthy about this, since whiskey was being made all over Ireland.

Some of the buildings in Locke's distillery are the oldest of their type in the country; those in the upper yard date from the eighteenth century. Unfortunately, all the old buildings at Bushmills were destroyed by fire in 1885.[9] In a physical sense therefore, Locke's can proudly claim to be the oldest surviving distillery in Ireland. If the existing distillery in Bushmills was established in 1784, then the Kilbeggan distillery can also claim to have the oldest licence.

In Kilbeggan the tradition is that a distillery was established on the site of the existing distillery in 1757. This claim is very plausible. There were three distilleries operating in Kilbeggan in 1782. The town lay within the Trim excise district, which had a total of 42 stills at this time. There had been 43 stills in the district in 1766;[10] it seems most probable that at least one of these was located in Kilbeggan, and at this stage it would have been in operation for only nine years.

From 1757, the fortunes of the distillery fluctuated over a period of two hundred years. Undoubtedly, the best years for the concern were during the last quarter of the nineteenth century. Thereafter, the management at Locke's was constantly short of capital and the plant was seldom overhauled. Much of the nineteenth-century equipment was still being used during the last distilling season in 1953. The bank called in a receiver five years later. Over the next decades the warehouses began to decay, until a new Irish whiskey company re-opened them in 1989 as bonded stores for maturing whiskey.

In the chapters that follow, the history of the distillery will be presented chronologically from 1757 up to the present. The surviving business records relate largely to the final decades of the distillery's history. A limited amount of sales books and wage books have survived from the nineteenth century. To trace a clear picture of the operation of the distillery back into the eighteenth century, it has been necessary to exploit a wide range of other sources, including deeds, maps, newspapers and parliamentary papers.

Business history is still in its infancy in Ireland. The limited amount of published work has generally focused on the giants of the Irish industrial sector, but Guinness and Harland & Wolff were not typical in terms of their scale and structure. This history of Locke's will provides a useful case-study of a company closer to the average-sized Irish business.

Though the distillery at Kilbeggan had a life which extended over and beyond the individuals who worked there at any given time, the fortunes of the business depended on two major factors. Firstly, the general economic conditions which governed the demand for whiskey. Secondly, the individuals who guided the activities of the company, from the purchase of corn, through the actual distilling process, to the marketing strategies which included advertising, transport logistics, etc. This book traces the gradual changes in the organization and structure of the distillery, which was intimately linked to the broader economic environment on one level. But on another level which was equally important, the distillery depended on the individuals who made the crucial planning and management decisions which enabled the business to react effectively to changing economic circumstances. The fortunes of the Locke family therefore depended on more than simply the ebb and flow of Irish economic activity.

Family networks were vital for business activity during the period of this study. Good marriages were critical for the Lockes, who rose during the second half of the nineteenth century from the ranks of the lower middle class to become one of the most prominent Catholic bourgeois families in Westmeath. The growing prosperity of the family, their social activities such as hunting and racing, their political and religious affinities, their marriages and relationships with the Protestant middle class, all provide us with a fascinating portrait of a successful Catholic middle-class family which challenges some of the stereotypes.

The taste of old Locke's whiskey can still be experienced by a privileged few who have access to what remains of the stock of the last distilling season. A few barrels and cases are still being stored in warehouses in Ireland and abroad. Locke's pot still whiskey from this era is quite distinct in taste from anything now produced by Irish Distillers in Midleton. Most of the brands sold today contain large amounts of patent still spirit which has a more neutral taste.

This whiskey is quite different to the Locke's whiskey, which was praised by people as different as Myles na gCopaleen and Winston Churchill.

Once more the aroma of whiskey hangs over the town of Kilbeggan as 20,000 barrels of pot still and grain whiskey mature in the old warehouses. On 17 July 1992 the first of these barrels was tapped and Locke's pure pot still single malt whiskey was launched onto the Irish market. A few ghosts must stir at the sight of the rolling barrels and the familiar sound of the coopers' hammers ringing around the distillery yard.

NOTES

1. E.B. Maguire, *Irish Whiskey* (Dublin 1973). R. Weir, 'The Patent Still Distillers and the Role of Competition' in L. Cullen and T. Smout (Eds), *Comparative Aspects of Scottish and Irish Economic and Social History of Ireland and Scotland* (Edinburgh 1974). R. Weir, 'In and Out of Ireland, The Distillers Company Ltd. and the Irish Whiskey Trade 1900–39'. *Irish Economic and Social History*, vol. 7.
2. A. McCreary, *Spirit of the Age, The Story of old Bushmills* (Belfast 1983).
3. Michael Byrne, 'The Distilling Industry in Offaly, 1780–1954' in Harmon Murtagh, *Irish Midland Studies* (Athlone 1980).
4. National Library Ms. 20,276 is a complete list of the surviving business records of John Locke and Co. which are held in the National Library. A smaller body of material is still kept at Brusna House, Kilbeggan, in the possession of Brian Quinn.
5. McCreary, p. 43.
6. *Journal of the Irish House of Commons*, vol. x, 1779–82, appendix dxxiii.
7. Maguire, p. 94.
8. J.P. Prendergast, *Calendar of State Papers, 1615–1625* (London 1880).
9. McCreary, p. 54.
10. National Library, J 3303–19 (Joly Pamphlets); *Observations on the State of the Distilling Trade* (Dublin 1782), p. 58. Journal of the Irish House of Commons, vol. x, 1779–82, appendix dxxiii. National Archives, m 5955, Return of the Number of Stills in Ireland, 1766.

1

BEGINNINGS
1757–1823

Kilbeggan is a small midlands town which lies fifty-six miles west of Dublin on the main Galway road. It is in the southern extremity of Westmeath, six miles north of Tullamore, which is just across the county border in Offaly. Today, the most prominent feature for the traveller passing through the town of Kilbeggan is Locke's distillery on the banks of the river Brusna. Since the distillery was established in 1757, the history of Kilbeggan has been inextricably linked with the production of whiskey.

The tradition of distilling in the midlands went back for centuries prior to the arrival of the Locke family in Kilbeggan. The concentration of the industry in the midlands at an early stage was mainly a consequence of the excellent quality of the barley and other corn grown in the region. The crumbling ruins of many large corn mills along the course of the river Brusna testify to its importance as a corn-growing area in the eighteenth and nineteenth centuries. As barley was (and still is) the primary raw material and the primary cost in the production of spirits, this was an important factor in bringing about the growth of the industry here.

Fuel in the form of turf was also available locally from the extensive peat bogs of the region. But after the canal branch was built in 1834, coal from both English and Irish pits could be used to fuel the fire under the stills at reasonable costs.

Water is a critical element for making good whiskey. This was drawn from the river Brusna, which flows down from

Lough Ennell through a limestone catchment area interspersed with peat bogs. This contrast between the limestone and peaty banks imparts a distinctive taste to the waters of the Brusna, which contributed to the unique character of the whiskey made in Kilbeggan. The art of the distiller brings together the various elements and ingredients (water, fire and corn) from which the spirit is drawn. Our knowledge of the evolution of this craft is still rather hazy and obscure.

It is impossible to be precise about exactly when distilling was introduced into Ireland. Although the consumption of ale and mead in Ireland goes back into prehistory, 'aqua vitae' and 'usquebaugh' begin to appear in the written sources only in the fourteenth century.[1] An ancient distilling worm was found in County Laois during the last century; an indication that the midlands was one of the early centres of the industry.[2]

The popularity of whiskey increased during the sixteenth and seventeenth centuries to such an extent that it began to alarm many English commentators on Irish life. Much of this comment was motivated by a fear that whiskey was helping to foster a spirit of recklessness and rebellion. Fynes Moryson, for example, was critical of the over-indulgent nature of the native Irish, yet he had a sneaking admiration for their whiskey. In 1617 he noted: 'Irish aqua vitae, commonly called usquebaugh, is held the best in the world of that kind, which is made also in England, but nothing so good as that which is brought out of Ireland.'[3]

English concerns about the extent of whiskey consumption in Ireland were tempered significantly by the potential revenue which it could yield to the crown. In 1556 the Parliament passed an act in Drogheda which made it illegal for anybody, with the exception of peers, gentlemen, and the freemen of the larger towns, to make aqua vitae without a license from the Lord Deputy.[4] To increase the revenue yield from the growing consumption of whiskey a duty of 4d a gallon was placed on all locally made spirits from 1661 onwards. To collect this tax on production the Crown was obliged to set up a new excise infrastructure; this was the first attempt to establish a civil department and it was from this rather ramshackle organization that the Board of Excise slowly evolved.[5]

From the early eighteenth century it is possible to get some idea from excise returns of consumer preference in Ireland. During the 1720s, when the population of Ireland was about 3 million, duty was paid roughly on 5.2 million gallons of spirits, 5.3 million gallons of beer and 12.4 million gallons of wine. In the 1790s, when the population had risen to about 4.5 million, duty was paid on 44 million gallons of spirits, 6.1 million gallons of beer and 15 millions of wine. The sharp increase in spirit consumption is quite apparent from these figures. Within the spirits category during this period, there was a major shift in consumer preference from imported rum, brandy and gin to Irish-made whiskey. Part of the explanation for this was rising customs duties imposed on imported spirits, which raised prices. In the 1770s 51 per cent of the spirits consumed was rum, whiskey accounted for 25 per cent, brandy 14 per cent and gin 10 per cent. By the 1790s, whiskey accounted for 66 per cent, rum 26 per cent, brandy 6 per cent and gin 1 per cent. There was a particularly sharp increase in whiskey consumption between the 1770s and the 1790s. Though these statistics exclude large quantities of spirits which were made illicitly, they still capture the dramatic growth in the popularity of whiskey during this period.[6]

In the early eighteenth century, spirit production and consumption in Ireland was more common in the north and east of the country and in the midlands. In the south, by contrast, wine, brandy, and rum were more common because of the growing trade of the southern ports with France, Spain and the colonies.

The growth in the output of the licensed distilling industry and the illicit trade over the course of the eighteenth century were both manifestations of the dramatic shift in consumer preference from imported spirits to those made in Ireland. The rising duty charges on imported spirits gave a degree of protection to the native industry, but improvements in the taste and quality of Irish whiskey was also an important factor.

Until the mid-eighteenth century distilling had predominantly been carried out in small stills. Distilling on a domestic basis was still common and it was not necessary at this stage to have a licence for a still of 12 gallons or under which was used for household consumption alone. From 1758, the minimum size still a licensed commercial distiller could use was 200 gallons. It is probable that many small household stills were used for commercial purposes, unknown to the excise authorities. It was only in 1761 that it became imperative by law for distillers to register the size and location of their stills with the local excise district collector.[7] Because of this registration law, it is possible to get an idea of the geography of the industry from a surviving register of 1766.

From this register (see table 1) it is evident that in the 1760s there was very little distilling in Munster. While there were a number of distilleries in Connacht, the main centres of the industry were in Ulster and Leinster. Leinster had the greatest number and the main concentration of these was in the midlands. There had obviously been significant growth in the mid-eighteenth century, when the first distillery in Kilbeggan was established. The distillers in this region registered their stills with the excise officers of the Athlone, Maryborough and Trim excise districts. Despite the rise in the number of stills nationally between 1766 and 1782, the number of distilleries in the midland excise districts actually fell from 183 to 151. The number of distilleries in the Trim district (of which Kilbeggan was part) fell from 43 to 33. Since there were three distilleries operating in Kilbeggan in 1782, it seems highly probable that at least one of these distilleries was operating in the town in 1757.

The first distillery in Kilbeggan was established in 1757.

TABLE 1
Return of Stills in Each Excise District in Ireland

	1766	1782		1766	1782		1766	1782
Armagh	65	74	Ennis	9	12	Naas		74
Athlone	46	44	Foxford	18	21	Newry		4
Baltimore	1	4	Galway	6	11	Ross		7
Cavan	94	39	Kilkenny	3	15	Sligo	26	6
Clonmel	9	47	Killybeggs	41	18	Strabane	46	72
Coleraine	45	39	Larne		14	Strangford	7	17
Cork Excise	3	8	Limerick	1	4	Tralee		1
Donaghadee	3	6	Lisburn	10	2	Trim	43	33
Drogheda	26	27	Londonderry	41	19	Waterford	1	4
Dublin Excise	63	52	Loughrea	7	21	Wexford	3	21
Dublin County	5	10	Mallow	3	20	Wicklow	2	10
Dundalk	24	24	Maryborough	94	74	Youghal	1	8

	1766	1782
TOTAL	746	876

Sources: National Archives, M 5955, List of Stills in Ireland 1766. *Journal of the Irish House of Commons* , vol. x, 1779–82, app. dxxiii.

At this time, the industry in general was expanding and commercial distilling was increasingly carried out in small distilleries, rather than in household stills. The early distilleries in Kilbeggan were small operations, catering mainly for local needs. The average output of the 42 distilleries operating in the Trim excise district in 1779 was less than 1800 gallons per annum. One hundred years later, Locke's itself would produce more whiskey per annum than all 42 distilleries operating in the Trim excise district combined in 1779.[8]

The 1757 distillery was probably run under the patronage of Gustavus Lambert, the most powerful landlord in the area and owner of the site of the distillery beside the Brusna. The Lambert family had acquired the dissolved Cistercian monastery and its lands in 1581 as Oliver Lambert had been an officer in the army of Lord Essex during the Elizabethan Wars. The stones of part of the first distillery came from the ruins of this monastery. The Lambert family retained their power base in the town as it expanded. In 1606 it became an incorporated market town and was granted a charter. Gustavus Lambert inherited the land which his family had acquired. Prior to this he had worked for the Board of Excise for a number of years and in 1746 was made the collector for the Trim excise district, a position he retained over the next decades. Between 1741 and 1753 he served as the member of parliament for the borough of Kilbeggan, succeeding his father, and between 1751 and 1760 he sat on the Grand Jury of Westmeath.[9]

Lambert was clearly a man with significant local political power, particularly in matters relating to excise. A distillery operating in his excise district need never have been reported to Dublin. He also sat on the Grand Jury for Westmeath and held the seat for the borough of Kilbeggan; so he could collect excise dues and keep the proceeds. This type of corruption was rife in Ireland at this time. Indeed many of the higher-ranking positions in the Board of Excise were given to Members of Parliament by the Lord Lieutenant in return for their support of measures which he wished to pass through the Parliament.[10] Support for government measures was blatantly bought in this fashion and Members of Parliament who acquired these positions considered it their right and privilege to be able to run the local excise as they pleased.

Initially the Kilbeggan distillery does not appear to have had a licence registered with the excise board in Dublin. If Lambert failed to report a new licence for the distillery established in Kilbeggan in 1757, there was nothing unusual in the fact; even low-ranking employees in the excise were often lax in this regard. In the neighbouring excise walk of Kinnegad in 1770, for example, the collector for the Trim excise district discovered that the gauger for that walk (the local supervisor and collector) had taken up licences which he had not accounted for and had pocketed the proceeds himself.[11] The whole procedure for remitting cash to the excise board in Dublin was enormously problematic for the excise authorities. Collectors were obliged to furnish accounts to the Accountant General on a regular basis but many were extremely negligent and there were long lists of collectors who had been dismissed or died with large sums still owed to the board. This situation got so out of hand that a new law was passed in 1765 whereby collectors who defaced or failed to deliver their accounts in order could face the death penalty for felony. The system ran much more smoothly after this.[12]

The minutes of the Irish Board of Excise during the 1750s and 1760s give the impression that Kilbeggan lay off the beaten track of the district's excise officers, who probably received their instructions from Lambert. There was no excise walk in the town at this stage but officials from Mullingar occasionally paid a visit to the region. In 1770, for example, the chief excise collector for the Trim district reported to Dublin that 'an Hogshead of whiskey had been seized near Tyrrels Pass for want of a permit'. But despite occasional forays into the district from Mullingar which resulted in the odd seizure, Kilbeggan appears to have been one of the many places in Ireland which the excise authorities seldom visited. There were over 1000 distilleries in the country at this stage and given the limited resources of the excise, total supervision of all of them was simply impossible.[13]

Excisemen were never among Kilbeggan's most popular visitors, but the town provided hospitality to many travellers passing along the main route from Dublin to the West. There is a good story still told about one of the more notable visitors during this period, Viscount Townsend, then the Lord Lieutenant of Ireland. Townsend was travelling through with his retinue in 1772; he never actually intended to stop in Kilbeggan but the wheel of his carriage broke nearby and he was obliged to stay overnight while it was being repaired. The inn he stayed in was run by the Cuffes, who as the saying goes were 'trying to pull the devil by the tail,' working day and night to make ends meet. Mrs

Cuffe was a great cook by all accounts and it wasn't long before his lordship was enjoying a large steak. In the meantime a bottle of the celebrated 'Kilbeggan Uisce Beatha' from the local distillery was opened. As the evening progressed a warm glow began to take possession of the Lord Lieutenant; such was his euphoria that he decided to confer the honourable order of knighthood on the humble innkeeper. By the next morning his mood had given way, and he was astounded at what he had done; he called the innkeeper aside and pleaded with him to forget what had come to pass the night before. The innkeeper replied: 'I could not agree with you more, your excellency, but Lady Cuffe won't hear of it'.[14]

An interesting aspect of the story is its depiction of the Protestant ascendancy momentarily dropping its guard while under the influence of whiskey. Social class distinctions temporarily vanish, and the world is turned upside-down. This theme recurs in Maria Edgeworth's novel, *Castle Rackrent*, which is set in the Irish midlands. When Sir Condy, the landlord, was out hunting, he often stopped at a particular cabin to drink whiskey out of an eggshell where he noticed the daughter of the distiller, Judy. While drinking whiskey punch at home he admitted to his servant, Thady (related to Judy), that Judy was worth twenty of Miss Isabella Moneygawll, his bride-to-be, and even made a vow to marry her.[15] Again, in this context, whiskey breaks down the religious and class divide.

Whiskey remained an exclusive drink until the last third of the eighteenth century; growing consumption during this period reflected a growth in the popularity of whiskey further down the social scale. The growth of distilling in Kilbeggan was closely connected with this rise in the demand for whiskey during the second half of the eighteenth century. By 1782 there were no fewer than three licensed distillers operating in Kilbeggan. One of them, Matthew McManus, was operating a still on part of the site where Locke's now stands. This was the distillery which had been established in 1757. McManus worked a still of 232 gallons' capacity in 1782. Like most small rural distilleries at this time, only one still was used, and the output would have been roughly 1500 gallons per annum. The income derived by McManus was probably insufficient for him to specialize in distilling; he was also renting land in the vicinity of Kilbeggan, and would have supplemented his income by farming.[16]

The site of this first distillery was on the west bank of the river Brusna on the south side of the road. It was an ideal industrial location and for many generations the water of the river had been exploited for industrial purposes. There had been a corn mill there since the seventeenth century at least.[17] Today a field on the south side of the road near the site is still called 'the bleach yard' from the 1770s when two merchants called Hill and Fleetwood rented the field for bleaching and finishing linen. Fleetwood built a pressing and dye mill on the site, but became a bankrupt at the beginning of the nineteenth century. The linen industry never flourished in Kilbeggan.[18]

There was a reduction in the number of distillers operating in the town from three in 1782, to one in 1796. During this period hundreds of small distilleries went out of business; the number of licensed distilleries in Ireland fell from 1152 in 1779, to only 214 in 1796. New regulations introduced in 1779 gradually wiped out many of the smaller concerns.[19] The Parliament took the view that a few larger distilleries could be more readily supervised than all the small distillers scattered across the Irish countryside. As the authorities had hoped, the industry became more concentrated in a smaller number of larger units. The recorded output of the licensed distilleries in Ireland almost trebled between 1780 and 1800, so initially the changes in the excise laws seemed to be justified.[20] However, many of the smaller licensed distilleries which closed were replaced by illicit operators, particularly in the north and west.[21]

In Kilbeggan, McManus was the only distiller still in

business by 1796. His distillery is clearly marked on the south side of the road on a lease map of 1795, and he is described as a distiller in another lease drawn up in that year. The capacity of the distillery had grown; the size of the still had been increased from 232 gallons in 1782 to 278 gallons in 1796.[22] Since the other distillers in the town had gone out of business, McManus had probably increased his trade.

The McManus family discontinued their association with the distilling industry before the end of the eighteenth century. It is not clear what precipitated this. Two of Matthew's sons, John and James, died, fighting on the side of the rebels in Kilbeggan in 1798. It is possible that one of the sons – or both – had been running the distillery. But a more probable explanation is that they simply switched to brewing, because it had become a more attractive business proposition.

In direct contrast to the experience of the distilling industry, government intervention in the brewing industry was considerably reduced in 1796. Taking the view that beer was the lesser of the two evils, the government removed the tax on it in 1796, while the tax on whiskey was raised. In these circumstances, a number of distillers simply converted into brewing. The McManus family established a brewery on the site of the first distillery around the turn of the century, and continued running it until 1846, when John Locke acquired the rights to the property.[23]

By the end of the eighteenth century, another distillery had been set up on the opposite side of the road to the McManus concern. It was established by the Codd family who had been involved in the region's malting trade, and who obviously believed there was still money to be made from the distilling industry, despite the major contraction in the number of distilleries all over Ireland. George Codd acquired the rights to this property through his marriage to Jane Gamble. Marriage often played a significant role in securing additional assets for industrial enterprises during this period. This was not the last time that a marriage would have an important influence on the future of the distillery. Jane had inherited a lease on the property on the death of her father in 1794. After her marriage to George Codd, their claim was consolidated when the owner, Francis Berry, granted Codd a new lease which enabled the Codds to retain control of the site over the next generation. The distillery established by William, George and John Codd was much larger than any which had previously been set up in the town, it had a 451-gallon still, but output was still small and probably never exceeded 3000 gallons per annum.[24]

The growth in the size of the distilleries operating in Kilbeggan conformed to a pattern which was occurring nationally. As the number of distilleries in Ireland declined dramatically in the last decades of the eighteenth century, the size of the few remaining distillers increased significantly as the industry became more centralized.

The buildings which the Codds erected at the end of the eighteenth century mark the first phase of development on the north side of the road. Still to be seen within the upper yard, they include the fine entrance to Locke's distillery. The old still house on the west side of the yard also dates from this period; the brickwork which originally supported the still and the receiver stand relatively intact. The much smaller scale of operations at this stage – relative to the late nineteenth century – is apparent from the size of this tiny still house. Most operations in the whole distilling process would have been carried out in this room at the end of the eighteenth century.

Typically, the pot still would have been used for heating the water for mashing. The mashing process would have been carried out in the same vessel using a manually operated oar. The pot still would also have been used for the brewing process and for fermentation. When fermentation was complete, the still would have been drained, cleaned, and the wash returned into it for the first distillation. After the low wines had been collected in the receiver the still was cleansed again and the distillate was passed through the still for the second run. The Irish used three runs through the stills while the Scottish used only two.

The Codd family distilling venture turned out to be a short-lived affair. By 1804, the whole concern had been converted into a brewery. For most of the first quarter of the nineteenth century there were two breweries operating on the site where Locke's distillery now stands (one on each side of the road).[25] Whiskey distilling temporarily ceased in Kilbeggan. It was a difficult time for small distillers to stay in business. During the 1790s the Irish Parliament had passed a number of acts which encouraged brewing at the expense of distilling, particularly the 1796 act which removed the tax on beer. These seem to have had the desired effect as the number of distilleries continued to fall. By 1823 there were only 40 distilleries left in the whole country. An important factor in this drop in demand for legally manufactured whiskey was the sharp rise in excise duties during this period. The first major rise was in 1801, followed by further increase in 1806 and 1816.

Beer was beginning to displace spirits in many parts of the country. In 1801 Coote noted that the demand for spirits had been declining throughout neighbouring King's County (Offaly) as people increasingly turned to beer and strong ale as substitutes.[26] We can safely assume that the same thing was happening in Westmeath. This would explain the switch from the production of spirits to beer in Kilbeggan.

Because the exceedingly tough excise legislation on spirit production forced many small distillers out of business between 1780 and 1823, the spirit supply came from either the few remaining distilleries in the larger towns or the illicit industry. It was only in 1823 that the government decided to curb the thriving illicit industry and improve the lot of the smaller licensed distiller. Firstly, the duty on spirits

TABLE 2
Excise Duty Charged on Spirits in Ireland
(per imperial Gallon)

1791	1 shilling	1.25 pence
1796	1 shilling	5.25 pence
1801	2 shillings	4.5 pence
1806	4 shillings	1.5 pence
1811	2 shillings	6.5 pence
1816	6 shillings	1.5 pence – 5 shillings 7.25 pence
1821	5 shillings	7.5 pence – (1823 dropped to 2s 4.75d)
1826	2 shillings	10 pence
1831	3 shillings	4 pence

Source: British Parliamentary Papers, 1834, vol. XXV, app. 22.

was significantly reduced. Secondly, excise intervention and surveillance of the distilling process were reduced and revised to become less oppressive on the interest of the distiller. The excise no longer interfered with the process unduly, and limitations on the production options of the distiller were removed. They could now make as little or as much as they wished and were taxed on sales rather than production, which reduced the amount of capital tied up in stock. These progressive legislative changes made distilling a more attractive business proposition.

After the overhaul of the excise laws in 1823, a number of new distilleries were established. The re-emergence of Kilbeggan as a centre of the distilling industry conformed very much to this revival in the industry all over Ireland.

NOTES

1. E. Malcolm, *Ireland Sober, Ireland Free; Drink and Temperance in Nineteenth Century Ireland* (Dublin 1986), p. 1.
2. John Feehan, *Laois* (Stradbally 1983), p. 336.
3. Malcolm, p. 3.
4. S. Morewood, *History of Inebriating Liquors* (London 1838), p. 619.
5. E.B Maguire, *Irish Whiskey* (Dublin 1973), p. 98.
6. Malcolm, pp. 22–3.

7. Maguire, pp. 105–8. In 1763 the size and location of small stills for household consumption also had to be registered.

8. The average output for the Trim district was calculated from National Library, Ir 381, 02, *Observations ... on the distilling trade in Ireland* (Dublin 1782).

9. Mullingar Library, Typed document, Information regarding the Lockes of Kilbeggan; J. Sheehan, *South Westmeath* (Dublin 1978), p. 393; *The Grand Juries of Westmeath, 1727–1853*, vol. 1.

10. Maguire, pp. 66–7.

11. PRO London, Cust 1, 117, Board of Excise Minutes; K. Connell, *Irish Peasant Society* (Oxford 1968), p. 36.

12. Maguire, p. 83.

13. PRO London, Cust 1, 114, Irish Excise Minutes, p. 9.

14. This story appears in the Ross School Collection 1837–8, vol. 732, Folklore Commission, UCD.

15. M. Edgeworth, *Castle Rackrent* (London 1964 ed.), pp. 27–8.

16. *Journal of Irish House of Commons*, vol. x, 1779–82, App. dxxiii. Registry of Deeds, Dublin, McManus to Locke, book 12, no. 174, 23 July 1846.

17. In 1682 there was a row of houses in this area called 'Mill Lane'. List of Occupiers in Kilbeggan, 1682. *Analecta Hibernica*, 1958, vol. 20, p. 207. I would like to thank John Mc Hugh for drawing my attention to this.

18. Registry of Deeds, Dublin, Hill to Fleetwood, vol. 362, p. 66, no. 242323.

19. Connell, p. 36, National Library, J. 3303–3319, *Observations .... on the Distilling Trade in Ireland* (Dublin 1782); *Journal of the Irish House of Commons*, vol. xvi, 1795–6, app. ccclxxvi.

20. Statistics Given Before the Committee on Public Houses, Journal of the House of Commons, vol. 1, 1855, p. 44.

21. Connell, pp. 36–7.

22. Lease map in possession of Doctor Sullivan of Kilbeggan (dated 1795); Registry of Deeds, 516, no. 338064, p. 446, Smith to Mc Manus; *Journal of the Irish House of Commons*, vol. x, 1779–82, app. dxxiii, vol. xvi, 1795–6, app. xxxvi.

23. Pigots Directory 1824; Slaters Directory 1846; deed, McManus to Locke, 1846 (possession of Bernard Mc Evoy for Cooley Distillery).

24. Registry of Deeds, Codd to Fleetwood, 581, 47, 388698, British Parliamentary Papers, 1823, vii, app. 33, Inquiry into Revenue Arising in Ireland.

25. There were no licensed distilleries operating in the town by 1807, neither were there any listed in the parliamentary return of 1823. Maguire, p. 365, British Parliamentary Papers, 1823, vii, Inquiry into Revenue Arising in Ireland.

26. A. Shipkey, 'Problems in Alcoholic Production and Controls in early Nineteenth Century Ireland', *The Historical Journal* vol. xvi, 2, 1973. M. Byrne, 'The Distilling Industry in Co. Offaly, 1780–1954', in H. Murtagh, *Irish Midland Studies* (Athlone 1980), pp. 213–14.

2

EARLY HISTORY
1823–1843

In contrast to the licensed distilling industry, illicit distilling flourished in Ireland between 1780 and 1823. The extortionate nature of excise legislation, supervision and duty payments led to the closure of many licensed concerns. The void left by these closures was readily filled by the illicit trade, which developed an extensive production and marketing network throughout Ireland. Westmeath was not one of the important centres for the production of illicit spirits, but by the beginning of the nineteenth century it had become an important market for illicit whiskey made elsewhere in Ireland. Although we have no detailed description of the illicit trade in the region (since it was an activity where people took care not to be noticed), its existence can be inferred from local folklore and other sources. When Barnard visited the town in 1886 he perceptively recorded a story about the local excise which probably comes from the first quarter of the nineteenth century:

Along the valley in olden times many smugglers were wont to locate, who gave a great deal of trouble to the excise officers. At Mabrista, a secluded nook near the distillery, formerly lived one 'Mooney', who carried on his nefarious practises under the very nose of the excise people. On one occasion a raid was about to be made upon him; Mooney, seeing in the distance the officers coming, called out to his wife to hide the three kegs of whisky in the garret. The ready-witted woman placed them in the middle of the floor, and then brought up her feather bed, which she ripped open, and completely covered the kegs. After searching all the rest of the house, the captain of the party entered the garret, and seeing nothing but a huge heap of feathers, called in his men that there was nothing in the d——d old cockloft but feathers, and it was useless to spoil their clothes by removing them.[1]

Irish folklore is rich with stories of how the illicit traders outwitted the excise men. Among a large part of the population, high duties and the whole excise infrastructure was generally perceived as another form of oppression and there was plenty of sympathy for the illicit traders, which made life difficult for the excise authorities.

After numerous official inquiries, the government realized that the existing excise legislation was penalizing the licensed industry and giving the illicit traders the upper hand. They also realized that the revenue yield from the hard-hit licensed industry was not reaching its full potential. In order to curtail the extent of the illicit industry and to improve the lot of the licenced distiller, the excise laws were entirely revised in 1823.

From then on, licensed distillers paid duty on the amount they made, rather than on what the excise calculated they could make. In order to counteract evasion, the old method of imputing output was generally assumed to be the maximum that could be produced from the still the distiller possessed. To make a profit under this system, distillers had to produce rapidly large amounts of spirits, which led to inadequate fermentation and a deterioration in quality. This system was particularly damaging to the smaller rural distillers because it was not worth increasing their output to supply the limited markets they served, unlike the big distilleries in urban locations, which had sufficiently large markets to profit from increasing their output.

The new legislation improved things for the smaller licensed distillers in particular, as they could now make their spirits more slowly and in whatever quantity they wished. Thereafter, they could store their stocks in bonded warehouses and duty became payable only when the spirits were sold, which reduced the capital tied up in stock. This led to a period of major investment and growth in the industry; the number of distilleries in Ireland rose from 32 in 1821 to 90 in 1837. The output of the licensed industry in the same period rose from 3,627,332 to 11,809,603 gallons.

TABLE 3
The Number of Distilleries in Ireland & Total Output and Exports (in proof gallons), 1821–62

	NO. OF DISTILLERIES	GALLONS DISTILLED	EXPORTS*
1821	32	3,627,332	293,973
1824		6,361,248	445,759
1825		8,835,027	789,886
1826		9,046,959	822,856
1827	82	7,283,317	541,521
1828	81	9,725,259	701,238
1829	80	9,208,538	782,193
1830	79	8,694,742	315,132
1831	81	8,786,341	1,214,817
1832	84	9,260,920	1,151,344
1833	82	9,509,774	601,033
1834	89	9,370,343	362,130
1835	93	11,167,580	536,795
1836	90	11,894,169	363,712
1837	90	10,980,910	341,789
1838	87	11,064,820	286,028
1839	89	10,254,591	369,827
1840	86	7,281,429	
1841	75	6,359,124	
1842	70	5,315,090	
1843	64	5,550,706	

*exports 1826–39 to England only.

Sources: British Parliamentary Papers, 1840, xliv, account of spirits exported from Ireland. 1851, liii, Return of spirits taken from bond for export; 1852-3, xcix, Return of spirits distilled in Ireland; 1863, lxvii, Return of distilleries in Ireland. W. Coyne, *Ireland, Industrial and Agricultural* (Dublin 1902). J. Nettleton, *The Manufacture of Spirits* (London 1895).

The industry now recovered in Kilbeggan. The 1820s and the 1830s were the first pronounced phase of expansion at the Brusna Distillery (as it was now called). The duty on spirits was re-duced in 1823 by more than half, from 5 shillings 7.5 pence to only 2 shillings 4.75 pence (see table 2, page 19), prompting a major growth in demand for legally made spirits. This made increased investment in the industry an attractive proposition, as is evident from the rise in the number of licensed distilleries in Ireland, and a corresponding rise in total output (see table 3). Exports of spirits from Ireland were negligible at this stage, so home demand provided the basis for this phase of expansion. As the excise had hoped, this growth was largely achieved by the licensed trade increasing its market share at the expense of the illicit trade.

The revival of the distilling industry in Kilbeggan during the 1820s must be seen in the context of the recovery of the legal industry all over Ireland. Very shortly after the licensing laws had been changed, a new distilling partnership was set up in Kilbeggan which brought George Codd's distillery back into production. A large new building was erected with frontage onto the river, so waterpower could be harnessed, which was necessary because the scale of production was significantly larger than it had been at the turn of the century.[2]

After the death of George Codd in 1823, his widow, Jane, let the buildings (which were then being used for brewing) to John Fallon. Fallon was an enterprising individual who was responsible for initiating the first phase of development at the Brusna Distillery. He was a tobacconist from Tullamore with limited financial resources. In order to acquire the use of the property and make it suitable for the production of whiskey, he sought financial assistance from his brother Charles, who was also a tobacconist, based in Mullingar.

The Fallons invested in improving the buildings, and installed new copper vessels and other equipment. Initially, Fallon continued to use the premises for brewing, but prospects within the distilling industry had now improved considerably and the concern was therefore converted back into a distillery. In order to increase the capital stock of this venture, Fallon entered into a new partnership in February

1824 with Patrick Brett of Clara and Henry Gower of Dublin. Fallon had already spent £500 on copper vessels, brewing pans, utensils, timber, machinery, horses, drays, barrels, other vessels and improvements to the buildings. In view of this, the new partners agreed to invest £500 each in the partnership. The company, therefore, started out with a joint stock of £1500 trading as 'John Fallon, Patrick Brett and Co'.[3]

Most industrial companies in Ireland at this time operated with limited capital resources. Fallon, Brett and Co. was typical in this respect. The Anonymous Partnership enabled the partners to pool their modest capital resources and establish a distillery which was economically viable. When production was resumed in the mid-1820s, output was about ten times greater than it had been at the end of the eighteenth century. During the 1825–6 season 'Brett and Fallon' produced 29,554 proof gallons of whiskey.[4] It wasn't long before the Brusna Distillery had renewed its reputation for fine whiskey, serving a market which was almost entirely confined to Westmeath and Offaly.

In order to diversify, the partnership set up a corn mill in the distillery which was also used for grinding malt and corn into grist for the mash. To make these improvements, John Whitfield was brought into the partnership in 1828. The output of the distillery was increased during the second half of the 1820s to exploit the growing demand for whiskey in the region. This resulted in a rise in the capital requirements of the company. When Fallon ran into major personal financial difficulties the shortage of capital became so acute that the partnership finally had to be dissolved in 1831.

In the following year, the fate of the business was saved when a new partnership was drawn up between William Codd, William Cuffe (both of Kilbeggan) and Patrick Brett. The significant growth of the distilling industry in Ireland during these years was obviously apparent to the partners and encouraged them to revitalize and extend the business. Codd and Brett were granted a new lease in 1832, and the joint stock of the company was raised further to £3300. The buildings and plant were valued at £2300, so the working capital of the partnership accounted for about a third of the company's joint stock.[5] This new arrangement seemed to place the Brusna Distillery on a better financial footing and it enabled the company to exploit the growing market for spirits during the 1830s.

The new partnership agreed to stay in business for fourteen years. They also decided that a certain amount of the profits should be reinvested in the business, the most common way of increasing the fixed capital investment in Irish industries at this time. Regular accounts were to be kept of

all the transactions and things relating to [the] said concerns [and] that William Codd party thereto should act as cash keeper and keep the cash and cash accounts of the said concerns and reciting that on the tenth day of October and on every succeeding tenth day of October during the continuance of the said partnership a full and general account should be kept, made up and take all and every the stock in trade, cash, bills and notes, debts and expences then [in] hands and due and owing to the said co-partnership and of al such debts engagements as should be found to the said co-partnership, by any such persons or persons by reason of the business of the said co-partnership, and a final balance struck on every tenth day of October in each and every year during the continuance of said co-partnership and the net proceeds shall on the tenth day of November in every year be divided between the said parties.[6]

This improvement in the book-keeping procedures is an interesting example of the growing importance attached to accounting, which was becoming a more specialized activity. The partnership had probably learnt from the financial problems of its predecessor, whose accounts had been more loosely arranged. The new partnership was more successful. The company's finances had been placed on a sounder footing which enabled the partners to profit from the boom in the Irish distilling industry during the 1830s. The output at Kilbeggan had already climbed up to over 40,000 proof gallons in the 1832–3 season (from under 30,000 gallons in 1825).[7] It probably rose over the following years, judging by the large increase in the duty paid in the Athlone excise district (of which Kilbeggan was now part). The collective output of the distilleries in this district rose from 153,902 in 1831 to a peak of 252,815 gallons in 1836.[8]

The partnership also benefited from the completion in 1834 of a canal branch from Ballycommon to Kilbeggan.[9] This was of vital importance to the future development of the distillery since it no longer depended for its trade on the immediate hinterland of the town. The canal branch linked Kilbeggan into the whole Grand Canal system. Kilbeggan whiskey could now be delivered cheaply to any point on the canal network, which linked up with Limerick via the Shannon, with all the locations on the Barrow and, most importantly, with Dublin. Because of the canal link and the high quality of the whiskey produced at the Brusna Distillery, the reputation of Kilbeggan whiskey slowly began to spread to other parts of Ireland. Another significant advantage of the link was that British coal could be imported via Dublin into the canal harbour in Kilbeggan at very reasonable rates. Prior to this, turf was used because it was cheaper than bringing coal overland to the distillery. But once the canal branch had been built, transport costs were substantially reduced and coal thereafter became the favoured fuel.

Because of the growth in demand during the 1830s, the company invested in improving the distillery and corn mill. Around 1840, a new millrace was built on the Brusna to provide a stronger current to the distillery waterwheel, thereby increasing the available motive power. The old arrangements for generating power had become insufficient for the needs of the expanding business.[10] An engineer writing about the drainage provided by the Brusna in 1844 noted the changes which had been made to the river:

About Kilbeggan the course of the river has been much and prejudicially interfered with; the race by which the water is brought to the distillery is at one place carried over the river course itself, which is passed under the head-race, by a small double culvert, having two five feet openings. Again at the town, two of the arches of the bridge are stopped up by the distillery works; the remaining three arches afford a waterway of only twenty-four feet six inches ... the piers and abutements of the three arches open to the river will require to be underpinned; and if the distillery works which have been erected within the last three years are to remain, an additional arch at the east end of the bridge will be required'.[11]

From this report it is apparent that the new millrace was dug between 1840 and 1843. The report casts a little light on the conflicting needs of the landowners who depended on the river for drainage, and the millers and other industrial interests located on the Brusna who wished to improve their power supply by erecting weirs. The engineer had to reconcile these conflicting interests but he seems to have been reasonably sympathetic to industrial interests on the river. He noted that 'few of the minor rivers of Ireland have their accessible natural falls so fully and usefully occupied', pointing out that there were four large mills, a distillery, and several oatmeal mills in the ten-mile stretch of river between Ballynagore and Clara.[12] These milling concerns and the distillery were important to the local economy; they provided a market for the wheat, oats and barley of the district, they provided employment and their owners made handsome profits.

The Kilbeggan partnership did a good trade during the 1830s, benefiting from the rise in the consumption of legally manufactured whiskey in Ireland. The high and rising levels of spirit consumption (both illicit and legal) over the previous decades had raised considerable alarm among the Protestant middle class. The quantity charged with duty in Ireland rose from over 9 million gallons in 1825 to over 12 million gallons in 1836. Whiskey consumption in Ireland reached record levels in the late 1820s and the mid-to-late 1830s. The reform in the excise laws of 1823 had enabled 'parliament whiskey' to regain a large part of the market which had been lost to the illicit poteen-makers.[13]

Despite the growing market share of the licensed industry, the illicit trade continued to thrive during the 1820s and 1830s. According to a deputation of Dublin distillers interviewed in 1834, illicit whiskey was sold in that city 'as openly in the streets as they sell a loaf of bread, and nothing is more publicly sold in the streets of London than illicit whiskey is sold in Ireland'. A similar situation existed in many other parts of the country, including Westmeath. A Presbyterian clergyman from Belfast interviewed in the same year thought that private distilling had never been worse; an employer he knew informed him that in ten years in trade, 'he never had a man in his employment by whom he did not lose money on account of their drunkenness', except for one who didn't drink. Per capita consumption of spirits in Ireland during the 1830s averaged well over 1.12 gallons per annum (which is the figure for 1831). This level of consumption was extremely high; Poland had the highest level of per capita consumption in the world for spirits in 1975 with a figure of 0.88 gallons per annum. The Irish figure for 1831 (which was higher than England or Scotland in absolute terms) doesn't even take into account the illicit industry; according to informed contemporary opinion this was even greater in some years than the output of the legal industry. In the 1830s there were more than seven times as many detections of illicit stills by the excise authorities in Ireland as in the rest of the UK put together.[14]

The statistics given above indicate that Ireland in the 1830s was a country which was quite literally sodden with drink. It is against this background that the dynamic growth of the industry both in Kilbeggan and in Ireland as a whole becomes explicable. The meteoric rise of the Temperance Movement at the end of the 1830s can also be understood as a reaction to this over-indulgence in alcohol.

By the end of the 1830s the market for whiskey was beginning to decline as both the Temperance Movement and economic depression rapidly began to reverse the high levels of spirit consumption. Father Matthew's campaign had a strong populist appeal among the Catholic middle class and the peasantry, unlike earlier campaigns which had been fostered by the Protestant clergy. Since the Catholic middle class and the peasantry were the main consumers of Kilbeggan whiskey, the good trade which the Brusna distillery had enjoyed during the 1830s came to an end. This downturn coincided with another problem; in 1838 Brett died and his wife, Maria, had to be paid £1000 for his share in the partnership.[15] This provided problems for the company's cash flow. To counteract this, Codd and Cuffe opened an account with the Moate branch of the National Bank, which advanced them a cash credit of £3000. Apparently however, even this was insufficient as Codd and Cuffe sought to extend their credit to £5000.[16] While part of this money was needed for the working capital of the company (to buy corn, pay wages, etc.), the partnership was still trying to expand the capacity of the distillery. In view of the slump in the industry, the increase in the fixed capital investment in the distillery was a bad decision which ultimately spelt trouble for the partnership, who obviously envisaged only a short term fall-off in demand.

The confidence of the partnership was ill founded. The boom years in the distilling trade had come to an end by the 1840s. The amount of spirits produced legally in the Athlone excise district plummeted from 224,217 proof gallons in 1838 to only 94,389 proof gallons in 1841.[17] Codd and Cuffe was one of the many companies that ceased distilling during this downturn and the partnership which had reaped healthy dividends during the 1830s was terminated. By 1843, the distillery was in a state of disrepair. It was at this point that the Locke family arrived in Kilbeggan.

NOTES

1. A. Barnard, *The Whisky Distilleries of the UK* (1887), pp. 392–3; K. Connell, *Irish Peasant Society* (Oxford 1968), p. 13.
2. 6 Inch Ordnance Survey, 1840 (Kilbeggan surveyed in 1837).
3. Pigots Directory, 1824, Registry of Deeds, Dublin, Anonymous

Partnerships, vol. 2, no. 428, 20 February 1924, Fallon to Fallon, 90, 562669, 12 September 1827.

4. British Parliamentary Papers, 1831, vol. xvii, Return of gallons of wash distilled in GB and Ireland.

5. Registry of Deeds, Book 12, no. 86, Brett, Codd, Cuffe.

6. *Ibid.*

7. E.B. Maguire, *Irish Whiskey* (Dublin 1973), p. 365.

8. British Parliamentary Papers, 1840, vol. xliv.

9. V.T.H. and D.R. Delany, *The Canals of the South of Ireland* (Plymouth 1966), p. 232.

10. Ordnance Survey 1841; Cuffe to Locke, 1843 (deed in possession of Bernard Mc Evoy for Cooley Distillery).

11. National Library, P. 210, J. Mac Mahon, *Report of the Commissioners on the Proposed Drainage of the Brusna* (Dublin 1844), pp. 14, 17.

12. *Ibid.*

13. E. Malcolm, *Ireland Sober, Ireland Free* (Dublin 1986), pp. 54–5, 324; Maguire, p. 286.

14. Connell, pp. 13, 23; Malcolm, pp. 323–4.

15. Registry of Deeds, Dublin, 1838, Book 7, no. 262.

16. Registry of Deeds, Dublin, Book 22, no. 202, 6 December 1839, Codd to Reynolds.

17. British Parliamentary Papers, vol. xliv, 1840, vol. xxxix, 1842.

3

THE TWO JOHN LOCKES
1843–1868

The Lockes had little wealth or status prior to their arrival in Kilbeggan. They were one of many middle-class Catholic families in Ireland whose wealth and social status rose dramatically during the second half of the nineteenth century. The limited degree of industrial development in Ireland during this period has been generally associated with Protestant interests, notably in the north-east around the industrial city of Belfast. This generalization does not hold in alcohol-related business ventures. Catholics had a very strong presence in distilling and brewing, and also in retailing alcohol in its various forms. The Lockes entry into the distilling industry is just one example of the Catholic predilection for this area of business.

The first distillery John Locke became involved with was in Tullamore; he ran this small concern for a few years in the late 1830s before moving on to Kilbeggan. Prior to the Tullamore venture, he had been a small merchant in the town of Monasterevin in Co. Kildare. He also did some farming on a small scale, leasing a small amount of land in Ballyboy, in neighbouring King's County (Offaly).[1] However, his income from farming and from various small-scale trading activities was quite modest.

Good marriages played a critical role in elevating the social status of the Lockes during the nineteenth century. Around the turn of the century, John Locke married into the Smithwick family, who ran the well-known brewery in Kilkenny.[2] The Smithwick connection was maintained by the Lockes over the next century, primarily because a large part of the yeast for the Brusna Distillery continued to be bought from their brewery in Kilkenny. It is quite possible that it was his wife, Jane, who first encouraged John Locke to become involved in distilling, which held out greater prospects of success at this stage than brewing, in which her own family was engaged.

The family continued farming when they moved to Kilbeggan in 1843, renting about 60 acres of land in the neighbourhood in the townlands of Aghamore, Camagh and Meeniska. John Locke was fifty-eight years of age at this stage; his son (also called John) was thirty-six. Upon arrival in Kilbeggan, the family moved into a house on the Lower Main Street (no. 57). Two of John Locke's sisters also came to Kilbeggan in the early 1840s; Mary Anne moved into another house on the same Street (no. 3) and another sister, Catherine, became the schoolmistress in the town. Both of these sisters lived out the rest of their lives in Kilbeggan and were buried in the family grave in Durrow Church.[3] It is unclear exactly why they moved to Kilbeggan, but it seems probable that at least one of them was dependent on John Locke. Catherine's position as a school-teacher in the town provides a few more clues on the family's social background. She was obviously an educated woman, which suggests that in the past the family had been able to afford education for all the sons and daughters. But the necessity for her to work suggests that the family's means were limited at this stage.

The Lockes first became involved in distilling during the boom of the 1830s. John Locke was well aware of the potential of the industry, having lived close to the thriving distillery in Monasterevin.[4] At the end of 1838, he answered an advertisement in a local newspaper seeking either a partner, or somebody to take over entirely a distilling concern in Tullamore.[5] In April of 1839, he began operating this distillery. Unfortunately, it turned out to be a sluggish venture, as the trade was then experiencing a downturn. John Locke was able to extract himself from any commitments he had made without significant financial loss. Early in 1840 the owner agreed to break the lease 'in consequence of the great falling off in the distilling trade'.[6] Unlike many distillers during this recession, Locke lived to fight another day.

After the failure of the Tullamore venture, it was surprising that John Locke became interested in running a distillery at Kilbeggan, especially in view of the depressed state of the distilling trade in the early 1840s.[7] The number of distilleries in Ireland fell drastically during this recession from 94 in 1838 to only 61 in 1844. As things turned out, his judgment proved to be sound. This was an early demonstration of his business acumen and tenacity in the face of a major recession in the industry. Since Codd and Cuffe's partnership had been terminated during this recession, they offered Locke favourable terms. The inventory of the distillery in 1843 (see appendix 1) indicates that investment over the preceding decades had turned it into a well-furnished distillery and mill. But some of the concern was in a state of disrepair when Locke took over. He was allowed a £50 reduction off the first year's rent of £200, in order to put a slate roof over the stills and to make other repairs.[8]

It is interesting to note at this point that the Tullamore connection was re-opened in the late 1980s when Cooley Distillery purchased the pot stills of the Williams distillery in Tullamore. These were moved to Kilbeggan. In 1990, Cooley also bought a large bonded warehouse in Tullamore which had previously been used by the Williams.

The relationship between the Lockes and the local community was reasonably good. Catherine Locke probably taught many of the distillery workers' children which would have strengthened the connection between the family and the townspeople. Very quickly the Lockes gained respect locally and assumed a higher social status than when they had lived in Tullamore and Monasterevin. Fortunately the distilling industry was beginning to recover by the time new whiskey came on line at the Brusna Distillery.[9] Unlike the Tullamore venture, the timing of Locke's entry into the market was more fortuitous in the case of Kilbeggan, and the family's future in the industry was therefore secured.

Drinking at work was common at this time in Ireland, particularly among tradesmen in the larger towns. Invariably in a distillery where there was access to large quantities of raw spirit, the habit was extremely prevalent. This could have serious consequences. In June 1845, for example, one of the workers at the distillery (who was in a state of intoxication) was crossing a hot tub in order to 'right the valve on one of the stills'. He slipped and fell into the tub and survived for only a few agonising days in the infirmary in Tullamore.[10] This was the worst accident that ever occurred at the distillery. Drinking at work was not altogether frowned upon by the management at Locke's. Even during the 1940s the management continued the tradition of allowing the workers two grogs (a double whiskey) during the course of a day's work, though this was reduced to one in the final years of the distillery's history. Undoubtedly drinking became a problem for many families associated with the distillery, particularly during the nineteenth century. It is still said in Kilbeggan that the women of the town put a curse on the distillery because their menfolk were perpetually drunk.

John Locke was fortunate that the initial fervour and the rapid advance made by the Temperance Movement in the late 1830s and early 1840s was short-lived; many a resolute pledge was reversed after this, so that by the middle of the decade the industry was beginning to recover. Although consumption never regained the extraordinary levels reached in the 1830s, whiskey drinking was too deeply woven into the fabric of Irish life to be stamped out so easily. There were few aspects of Irish culture which were not heightened by whiskey. At births, weddings and funerals a drop at least (and often a great deal more) was considered to be an integral part of the proceedings. In pubs and shebeens whiskey was power for the cause. The relationship between the fiddler and his dancers, the story-teller and his audience, the matchmaker and his clients, were all assisted by whiskey. On Irish fair-days there were few dry bargains to be had. Although the number of distilleries continued to decline in the 1840s, Locke's managed to survive. There was still room in the market for a small distillery which made particularly fine whiskey.

When Locke arrived, which was being run by John and George Mullin, there was also an oatmeal mill in the distillery. Locke acquired the use of it only in November 1844. This four-storey mill had three stones driven by a large waterwheel. There was also a duster and four sets of elevators (one set for shelling, one for meal, one for raw corn and another for dry corn; see appendix 1). Diversification into milling was an important part of Locke's business between the 1840s and the 1860s, when distilling was not very remunerative. It is evident from the earliest surviving ledger that sales of grain, meal and malt were almost as important as sales of whiskey. The entries in this ledger confirm that in the late 1840s (and presumably before this) the business was local. There was very little trade with Dublin, but a few customers in the nearby towns of Tullamore, Clara and Moate.[11]

The earliest surviving business record of the company dates from November 1848. It refers to a consignment of oatmeal to Tullamore for outdoor famine relief and the workhouse.[12] Right from the beginning of the Famine years, when many of the poorer families in Kilbeggan suffered from hunger and privation, John Locke made generous donations to the Kilbeggan Relief Fund. He gained a reputation for his benevolence towards the poor of the town during these difficult years, giving out large quantities of oatmeal and soup, in addition to clothing and money. The Locke family retained this reputation over the next generations, contributing to the general welfare of the town. John Locke the second, for example, became the chairman of Kilbeggan Dispensary Committee throughout the 1850s and during most of the 1860s.[13]

From an early stage the Lockes were known for leading an exuberant and racy social life. This would have assisted their integration into the social networks which were an important part of business life in the midlands. The Lockes were instrumental in establishing the Kilbeggan Races, which survive to this day and are still partially sponsored by John Locke and Co. Ltd. The family had a great love for horses. Hunting, racing and even polo were enthusiastically pursued by various members of the family, and became the main focus of their social life in the district. John Locke's early involvement with the races can be seen from the following notice, which appeared in the *Westmeath Guardian* and *Longford Newsletter* on 25 March 1847:

SPORTING INTELLIGENCE

To be raced for in the neighbourhood of
KILBEGGAN
On Wednesday the 14th April 1847
A SILVER CUP
value forty guineas; 20 Guineas to be added by the Stewards; best of heats. Two miles over a sporting country. The cup to be won three successive times; before it becomes the exclusive property of any individual. Weight for Age ... Three horses to start, or no Race – the winning horse to be sold for 80 Guineas, if demanded in the usual way by a Subscriber, within half an hour after the Race. Entrance – Two Guineas to Subscribers, or Three Guineas to Non Subscribers.
Same Day Over Same Course, Will Be Raced For,
A SILVER MOUNTED WHIP
Value Two Guineas,
To which will be added Five Guineas by the Stewards.
Weight for age ... Entrance for same, 10s. 6d, up to 10 o'clock the evening before, or double at the post.
The Horses for the Cup, to be entered on or before the 10th day of April.
STEWARDS
JOHN LOCKE, Esq.   WILLIAM CODD, Esq.
MARK KELLY, Esq.   JAMES CLARKE, Esq.

This was probably a good public relations exercise for the

distillery. There were (and still are) strong links between gambling and drinking. Few activities at this time would have drawn such large crowds across the class and religious divides as a day at the races.

John Locke initially leased the distillery in 1843 on a short-term basis. But in 1846 he signed a 999-year lease on 'the distillery concerns with the machinery and utensils ... and also the corn mill and premises with the machinery ... and also the plot of ground and turf yard at the rear of the distillery concerns together with a sufficient flow or fall of water to the distillery concerns, mill and premises from the River Brusna.' The yearly rent for the distillery was £250 sterling. On the same day, Locke took out another 999-year lease on the brewery, house, yard, lands and garden on the other side of the road for a yearly rent of £60.[14]

John Locke lived for only a few years after he had secured the rights to the property for his family. His wife, Jane, died on the 24 April 1848, and he was not long in following her; he died on 1 January 1849 at the age of sixty-four.[15] In the short time he had lived in Kilbeggan he had successfully established a business which would survive for another three generations.

The second John Locke was forty-two when his father died. He was still a single man at this stage, but married within a year to Mary Anne Theresa Devereux, who was twenty-three years younger than him. This was an extremely good marriage from the Locke's point of view. Her father was Nicholas Devereux,[16] who owned the Bishops Water Distillery in Wexford (the biggest one in the south-east). The Devereuxs were a wealthy and politically powerful family. Mary Anne's Uncle, John Devereux, was MP for Wexford in the 1840s and 1850s. Another brother, Richard Devereux, built a huge fortune from his Wexford-based shipping and malting business. He was a generous benefactor to the Catholic Church, building and endowing the Convent of Mercy at Summerhill among others. Mary Anne took after her uncle Richard in this respect; establishing the Convent of Mercy in Kilbeggan in 1879 with the assistance of her father. John Locke's marriage into the Devereux family was a strong reflection of the rapidly growing wealth and social status of the family after they had acquired the distilling and milling business in Kilbeggan.

The first child of Mary Anne and John Locke, Richard Joseph, was born in Kilbeggan at the beginning of November 1852.[17] A second son, John Edward, was born in 1854, and two years later she gave birth to her first daughter, Mary Josephine, who died when only a few months old.[18] This was followed by another tragedy in June 1857 when their eldest son died of scarlatina.[19] Her last child was born a few years later in 1860.[20] He was christened James Harvey; John Edward, the oldest surviving brother, and James Harvey were to be the two members of the family who became engaged in the distilling trade.

The family income continued to be supplemented by farming and milling. The distilling end of the business does not appear to have done very well during the 1850s and early 1860s. Judging by sales figures for the 1861–2 season (23,500 gallons), output at the distillery in that year was lower than it had been in the 1820s and 1830s.[21] The local demand for spirits was declining and competition from other midland distillers was beginning to erode Locke's market share. The income derived from milling and farming must therefore have been very important at this time. A number of smaller rural distilleries in Ireland closed during these years. A second smaller distillery in Kilbeggan, for example, located opposite Locke's on the east side of the Brusna, shut down;[22] the local market was simply not large enough to sustain a second distillery. Locke's did well to survive these decades.

From the earliest surviving Sales Day Book, it is possible to get some idea of Locke's market in the early 1860s. It is apparent that the distillery's market was still predominantly local: the bulk of the company's trade was in Westmeath,

TABLE 4
*Geographical Locations of Locke's Sales in the
1861–2 Season (number of sales made)*

Westmeath	269
Offaly	48
Roscommon	43
Dublin	37
Galway	8
Kildare	6
England	2
TOTAL	414

Source: National Library, Ms 20020, Sales Day Book 1861–71

Offaly and Roscommon. The growth of the Dublin trade was the first sign of the development of an extra regional market. This was to increase significantly as the decade proceeded.

The market in the vicinity of the distillery held out little prospect for the growth of the industry in Kilbeggan. Locke's needed to establish markets outside its immediate hinterland if the business was to survive in the changing circumstances brought about by the transport revolution. Many of the small distilleries depending entirely on local markets closed down during this period in the face of competition from larger distilleries in Dublin, Cork and Belfast. Locke's market began to broaden geographically during the 1860s. The transport infrastructure facilitated this development; the canal branch linked Kilbeggan with the Grand Canal system and the construction of the rail network opened up a second transport option. Kilbeggan was only four miles from Horseleap Station which was on the Midland and Great Western Railway, and Tullamore Station, which was seven miles away on the Great Southern and Western Railway. Access to these transport networks enabled Locke's to expand and survive during a period when the Irish distilling industry was becoming more centralized in a smaller number of larger distilleries.

Expansion during the second half of the 1860s can be inferred from two sources. In a General Entry Book which the Customs and Excise kept for the Kilbeggan district, a declaration signed by John Locke shows that new plant was being installed in 1867:

> I John Locke Distiller at Kilbeggan in the Parish of Kilbeggan and County of Westmeath do in addition to my former entry now make entry of one Still for distilling Low Wines and Feints into Feints and Spirits called no. 2 Low Wines Still marked L No. 87. One pipe and one cock for conveying Low Wines and Feints from the Low Wines and Feints Charger into the Said Still. One Worm belonging to said Still. One Pipe and Cock from arm of said Still for conveying the portion of spirits condensed in said arm and head of still. One pipe and cock for discharging the spent lees from said Still.
>
> As witness my hand the 17th day of December one thousand eight hundred and sixty seven.
>
> JOHN LOCKE
>
> Signed in my presence and received this 17th day of December 1867.
>
> FREDERICK OLIVE Officer.[23]

Obviously a new phase of fixed capital investment had begun at the distillery. This was long overdue since much of the plant would not have been changed since the previous phase of expansion in the 1820s and 1830s.

The increase in Locke's sales during the second half of the 1860s is also recorded in the company's Sales Day Book; by the 1869–70 season Locke's sales had risen to 59,469 gallons (compared to 23,500 in 1861–2). The company's whiskey was selling all over Leinster, notably in Dublin. Sales in the capital alone had risen to 24,685 gallons which was over 41 per cent of the distillery's total sales. Sales in Munster and Connacht were also increasing. In addition, the company was beginning to export whiskey to the larger industrial towns in England like Liverpool, Manchester and Bradford which had growing Irish populations at this time. Exports to England in the 1869–70 season amounted to 12,497 gallons, or 21 per cent of total sales.[24]

The output of the distillery by the end of the 1860s was

higher than it had ever been. The whole structure of the company had been radically overhauled during the 1860s. The Lockes obviously developed new business contacts and networks, particularly in Dublin and in England. These two destinations accounted for over 62 per cent of the distillery's sales by the end of the decade, and the major expansion at Locke's. Its market had changed radically from being rural (largely confined to Westmeath, Offaly and Roscommon) to being predominantly urban. Although we have already noted the importance of the transport network in facilitating this striking shift, there must also have been radical improvements in the company's marketing techniques.

John Locke (the second) died on 13 August 1868. His death occurred during a major phase of expansion at the distillery. The business was left in trust to his wife, Mary Anne, and their two sons, John Edward and James Harvey, aged only fourteen and eight respectively at the time.[25]

NOTES

1. Registry of Deeds, Dublin, 751, 326, no. 510862, 31 March 1820; National Library, Ainsworth Report no. 65; For the Smithwicks yeast connection see Ms 20138(2) and (3). Invoices from Smithwick and Sons 1950–3. Locke's also got yeast from Guinness.

2. Westmeath County Library, Mullingar; Information Regarding the Lockes of Kilbeggan (typescript document among various items relating to the distillery).

3. Gravestone of the family at Durrow Church; Griffiths Valuation for the parish of Kilbeggan; Slaters Directory 1846; National Library, Ms 20064, Farm Accounts 1868–78.

4. E.B. Maguire, *Irish Whiskey* (Dublin 1973), p. 364; J. Holmes, 'Monasterevan Distillery', *Journal of the Kildare Archaeological Society*, xvi, no. 4, 1969.

5. *Leinster Independent*, 1 December 1838.

6. Registry of Deeds, Pentland to Locke, Memorial book 3, no. 74, 4 February 1840, Locke to Pentland, book 10, no. 190, 13 May 1841.

7. British Parliamentary Papers, 1854, vol. Lxv, Number of Distillers in Ireland.

8. Cuffe to Locke, 1843 and 1846, Deeds in the possession of Bernard

Mc Evoy for Cooley Distillery.
9. British Parliamentary Papers, 1854, vol. lxv, Spirits consumed in Ireland.
10. *Westmeath Guardian*, 19 June 1845.
11. National Library, MS 20061, Miscellaneous Ledger, 1848–68.
12. *Ibid.*
13. *The King's County Chronicle*, 3 January 1849; National Archives, MS 8753, Relief Commission Kilbeggan, 1847; Offally County Library, Tullamore, Minute Book of the Committee of Management of the Kilbeggan District Dispensary Committee, 1852–.
14. Registry of Deeds, Cuffe to Locke, book 12, no. 173, 23 July 1846; Mc Manus to Locke, book 12, no. 174, 23 July 1846.
15. Family gravestone, Durrow church; *Kings Chronicle and Provincial Intelligencer*, 3 May 1848.
16. Family gravestone; Wexford Town Roman Catholic Baptismal Register, Mary Devereux, born 24 Sept 1831. I would like to thank Celestine Murphy of the Wexford County Library for a copy of this baptismal register; *The King's Chronicle and General Provincial Intelligencer*, 30 January 1850, names the late John Devereux of Dublin as her father. This seems to be a mistake.
17. *King's Chronicle and Provincial Intelligencer*, 3 November 1852.
18. *Ibid.*, 23 April 1856.
19. *Ibid.*, 17 June 1857. Another son was born at the beginning of August 1957, but nothing is known of what became of him. See *King's Chronicle and Provincial Intelligencer*, 5 August 1857.
20. Graveyard, Kilbeggan.
21. National Library, Ms 20020, Sales Day Book, 1861–71.
21. National Archives, Griffiths Valuation, vol. 4. 1752.
22. *Ibid.* Ordnance Survey 1840, Byrne, *op cit.*
23. General Entry Book, Kilbeggan District, 1867–1913.
24. National Library, MS 20020, Sales Day Book, 1861–71.
25. National Archives, Mullingar Will Book, 1859–74.

4

MARY ANNE LOCKE
1868-1880

After the death of her husband in 1868, Mary Anne Locke ran the distillery until about 1880, with the assistance of some of the senior employees of the company. Her signature appears in the Customs and Excise General Entry Book very soon after John Locke's death, and she continued to sign the many declarations of changes in the distilling apparatus in this book (which was a legal obligation) down to the 1880s. Walter Furlong, the head distiller and manager, seems to have played a significant role during this period in helping her to run the distillery.

The business continued to be managed in this fashion until such time as John Edward was old enough to take over. It is clear from the records that the distillery was being particularly well run during this period. We have already noted the growth in sales over a wider geographical area during the 1860s. The output of the company was also rising. The throughput of the brewing process almost doubled between 1865-7 and 1868-70, and the distilling season was extended.[1]

The continued expansion of the distillery after John Locke's death indicates that Mary Anne Locke was a shrewd women with good business sense. It is probable that her father, Nicholas Devereux – a capable distiller himself – advised her. Having grown up within a distilling family she was probably quite familiar with the whole business. She had also lived in Kilbeggan for almost twenty years at this stage so she was no stranger around the Brusna Distillery. A few months after her husband's death she opened a spirit store in the yard beside Brusna House 'for the purpose of Keeping and Storing Spirits for Sale as a Dealer'. This additional outlet was probably designed to sell small quantities of mature spirits to local households and publicans.[2]

Mary Anne's business acumen has largely been forgotten but her shrewdness has survived in the folklore of the town. There is a story that she did not always pay her dues to the excise since the odd barrel or two were kept in her own house away from the scrutiny of the excisemen. Suspecting this, the excise called at the house one night with a warrant to search the house. On seeing them knocking at the door from her bedroom upstairs, she quickly threw a blanket over the two barrels and placed a mirror on top of them, so that to all intents and purposes they looked like a dressing-table. She then sent her maid to open the door. As the excise men looked through the house she sat at this bogus dressing-table and combed her hair. After searching the whole house without success (including the room where Mary Anne was vacantly looking into the mirror combing her hair) the two excisemen had to leave the house feeling rather embarrassed for their troubles.

Distilling was a highly seasonal activity; malting and fermentation was generally undertaken between October and May, because the warm months were unsuitable for malting and fermentation.[3] This pattern can be discerned at Locke's from the average number of workmen employed per week during each month of the 1873–4 season (see table 5).

At the end of the 1860s attempts were being made to maximize the cost efficiency of the whole process by reducing overheads per period. This was done by increasing the number of distilling periods in a season, and extending the season. Pot still production is carried out in different runs; the whole process from the mashing to the final distillation is carried out in batches called periods within the industry. There were nine distilling periods during the 1866–7 season; in 1868–9 the number had risen to 18.[4]

From the estimates on table 6 it can be seen that the cost of labour (including salaries) came to under 9 per cent of total costs. Labour was slightly cheaper than fuel. Malt and grain accounted for over 74 per cent of total costs. Added value in the distilling industry was low. To make a reasonable profit it was necessary, therefore, to increase output considerably. This is exactly what the company did over the next decades.

Output at Locke's rose from under 60,000 gallons at the end of the 1860s to about 78,000 gallons in the mid–1870s. The decade between 1875 and 1885 was the most dynamic phase of growth in the distillery's history. By 1886 output had risen to 157,000 gallons per annum.[5] This growth took place while the distillery was under Mary Anne's management, and coincided with a period of expansion in the Irish distilling industry at large. Although whiskey sold under the Locke's label was gaining a more widespread appeal, some of the expansion was due to the increasing sales to blenders in both Belfast and England. The strong taste and heavy body of Locke's whiskey made it particularly suitable for giving life to more neutral patent still spirit. The growth of the British market for blended

TABLE 5
Average Number of Workmen Employed at Locke's in 1873–4

1873	OCTOBER	37
	NOVEMBER	41
	DECEMBER	42
1874	JANUARY	43
	FEBRUARY	42
	MARCH	43
	APRIL	43
	MAY	35
	JUNE	27
	JULY	21
	AUGUST	25
	SEPTEMBER	27
	OCTOBER	40

Source: National Library, Ms 20051, Workmen's Accounts 1873–6.

whiskey after the 1860s was particularly beneficial to the patent still distillers, who produced the lion's share of the blend, but good pot still whiskey was also required to give taste. The blenders usually bought the pot still whiskey they used from old established firms like Locke's, who therefore benefited from the growth of the trade in blended whiskey in the 1870s and 1880s. Initially, blended whiskey did not encroach on Locke's traditional markets for pot still whis-key in the south of Ireland, although this began to happen in the 1890s.

Considerable sums were spent during these years in improving the machinery and buildings at the distillery. From a general entry book kept by excise, which recorded in detail all the changes to the plant, it is evident that improvements and expansion continued throughout the 1870s and 1880s. The old works were completely overhauled and the business was reorganized to facilitate the increase in the distillery's output.

Expansion is also evident from the industrial archaeology at the distillery. A large amount of new machinery and plant was installed between the 1860s and the mid–1880s. Stamp marks on the pillars and brackets supporting some of the line shafting, and on the throw pumps, bear the name of E. Toomey, a Dublin firm. One of these pillars beside the still house also has the date '1871' beside Toomey's name.[6] It is probable that this company undertook the first major overhaul of the millwork at the distillery. Dublin was among the most important centres of the distilling industry in the United Kingdom at this stage, so there were a number of Dublin-based engineering companies servicing the needs of the industry. The pot stills at Locke's were made by Millar's of Dublin. The spent wash tanks were erected by Ross and Walpole of Dublin and two new worm tubs were installed in the first half of the 1880s by Strong and Sons of Dublin. By the 1880s some of the new machinery for the distillery was being made up by British companies. One of the three millstones which survives in

TABLE 6
Estimated Cost of Distilling in 1868

	£	%
Rent for 12 months	250	2.1
3 horses "	75	0.6
Interest & Discount on bill	240	2.0
Salaries	280	2.3
Labour	785	6.5
Fuel	1100	9.1
Candles & oil	35	0.3
Barm	100	0.8
Malt	2795	23.2
Oats	1820	15.1
Barley/Wheat	4344	36.1
Incidental Expences	200	1.7
SUB-TOTAL	12,024	100
Less sale of wash grain	960	
TOTAL	10,564	

Source: National Library Ms 20062 Miscellaneous Ledger, 1858–71.

the main building bears the stamp mark of 'Kay and Hilton, Bank Hall Bridge, Liverpool, 1878'. The underbacks and the washbacks were made up by a back maker (vat maker) employed at Locke's. A number of other tradesmen were employed on a fairly permanent basis, to carry out most of the continuing repairs at the distillery. There was a carpenter's shed and a forge for this purpose.[7]

It is probable that John Edward and James Harvey were becoming increasingly involved in the distillery from the mid–1870s onwards. John Edward was twenty-one in 1875, his younger brother, fifteen. A few years after the death of their father in 1868, Mary Anne, their mother, moved out of Kilbeggan with the whole family to Ardnaglue, a larger country house close to the town. This house, with a tree-lined avenue, was more in keeping with the rising social aspirations of the family. Their previous home was too close to the distillery to escape the constant pressures of the business. This was quite typical of middle-class residency patterns during this period. The growing income of the family during these years provided the funds for the purchase of the house and farm at Ardnaglue; the move brought major changes to their lifestyle.

Some of the profits from the distillery were used by Mary Anne to help establish the new convent in the town. The Lockes provided the land on which the Sisters of Mercy Convent was built; in addition Mary made a subscription of £1000 towards the buildings and subsequently made a munificent gift of between £5000 and £6000 to the nuns. Her grand-daughters, Mary Evelyn and Florence, laid the foundation-stone of the main building.[8] A picture of Mary Anne and her father Nicholas Devereux still hangs in the convent as a tribute to their generosity. The Catholic Church depended on the Catholic middle class for a large part of its building programmes. Donations from a successful entreprenurial family like the Lockes were not unusual.[9] But it is clear that Mary Anne was more generous than subsequent generations of the family, who were somewhat less pious and devotional in their lifestyle.

By the 1880s John Edward Locke had taken over the management of the distillery. He moved back to Brusna House, just across the road from the distillery[10] while James Harvey remained at Ardnaglue. In the following years the two brothers were partners in running the thriving distillery. It was during this period that the distillery reached peak output.

NOTES

1. National Library, MS 20062, Miscellaneous ledger, 1858–71.
2. General Entry Book, 1867–1913.
3. P. Mathias, 'Agriculture and the Distilling and Brewing Industries in the Eighteenth Century', *Economic History Review*, vol. 5, 1952, p. 249.
4. Ms 20062, *op cit*.
5. National Library, Ms 20020, Sales Day Book, 1861–71; A. Barnard, *The Whisky Distilleries of the UK* (1887 London), p. 394.

6. Toomey had been a foreman in Mallets large engineering works in Dublin before setting up in his own right. The surviving waterwheel at Kilbeggan is typical of many of the waterwheels which Mallets firm made and erected in Ireland (predominantly in Leinster). See R. Cox, *Robert Mallet 1810–1881* (Dublin 1982), p. 82; G. Bowie. *Watermills, Windmills ... in Ireland* (Unpublished PhD, Queen's University Belfast 1977), p. 27.

7. Barnard, pp. 393–4; General Entry Book for the Kilbeggan District, 1867–1913.

8. Slaters Directory, 1894; *Westmeath Examiner*, 29 August 1959.

9. E. Larkin, 'Economic Growth, Capital Investment and the Roman Catholic Church in Nineteenth Century Ireland', *American History Review*, vol. 72, 1967.

10. *King's County Chronicle*, 16 August 1883.

5

THE BEST YEARS: JOHN EDWARD AND JAMES HARVEY LOCKE 1880-1926

The growth of Locke's distillery between the 1860s and the 1890s must be seen in the context of the growth of the Irish distilling industry at large. Although much of this growth was related to the expansion of patent still production, some pot still producers also benefited from the growth of the export trade in blended whiskey to the growing English market.

The notable difference in the taste between pot and patent still whiskey is a consequence of the application of different distilling techniques. The traditional pot still is a flat-bottomed copper pot with a high head to prevent the fluid from boiling over. From the head runs the worm which carries the alcohol in the form of vapour through a spiral tube which is contained within a vessel of cold water that condenses the vapour into liquid. This liquid (called low wines) is redistilled, which makes it stronger. Patent still production, by contrast, is a continuous process and highly concentrated alcohol is produced in one run, so much less fuel is consumed. This revolutionized the economics of the industry. The low wines are not condensed and collected as in pot still production; instead the vapour passes on to a large rectifying column where it is purified into strong spirits. These spirits contain very little of the volatile oils produced from pot still production which give whiskey its flavour and character. This is why patent still whiskey is blended with pot still whiskey.[1]

Belfast became the most important location for patent

still production and the blending trade towards the end of the nineteenth century, while Dublin remained the traditional stronghold of the pot still industry. There is an element of truth in a comment by Lloyd George in 1915 that the perpetual disputes and investigations into the pros and cons of pot and patent still whiskey were in reality 'a fight between Belfast and Dublin'.[2]

The English market provided the demand for blended whiskey which enabled the Irish distilling industry to increase its output between 1860 and 1900. Exports of Irish whiskey rose from about 1 million gallons in the 1860s to almost 8.5 million gallons in 1907.[3] The number of distilleries did not increase much after the 1860s, but output rose from 4.8 million gallons in 1861 to over 14 million gallons in 1900.[4]

Though Dublin exports of pot still whiskey increased during the second half of the nineteenth century, the main growth in Irish exports came from patent still distillers based in Ulster (predominantly in Belfast). But Locke's were one of several southern pot still producers building up a small niche in the English market.

TABLE 7
Exports of Whiskey from Ireland 1860–1905 (gallons)

	BELFAST	DUBLIN	CORK	TOTAL
1860	135,270			1,267,478
1871	754,427	727,642	611,720	2,093,789
1876	2,006,383	1,281,708	613,564	3,901,655
1884	3,837,024	1,158,526	630,460	5,626,010
1892	4,885,056	1,701.258	598,152	7,184,466
1900	6,648,912	1,650,473	494,424	8,793,809
1905	5,262,057	2,003,316	212,625	7,477,998

Sources: BPP, 1861, vol. lviii, Return of spirits exported. Totals for 1871 to 1900 includes Belfast, Dublin and Cork only. These figures are converted into gallons from Belfast Harbour Commissioners, Cork Harbour Commissioners and *Thom's Directory*. The 1905 figures come from *Thom's Directory*.

In 1947 the secretary of Locke's stated that the company had 'built up a very large, old and valuable connection in England, some of that connection going back for fifty or sixty years'.[5] We have noted already that the beginnings of the English trade actually went back into the 1860s: by the end of that decade Locke's exported 21 per cent of its total sales to England, notably to Liverpool, Manchester and Bradford. Much of the trade to England and Ulster went to blenders, whose product was more popular in Britain than the more expensive pure pot still whiskey favoured in the south of Ireland.[6]

The increase in the export trade reversed the decline which the Irish distilling industry had experienced during the 1850s and early 1860s. The number of distilleries in Ireland fell from 51 in 1851 to only 22 by the mid–1860s. Thereafter the number of distilleries remained fairly stable and output rose significantly. Most of the distilleries which closed during the 1850s and early 1860s were those which had poor access to the transport network and depended on limited local markets. Locke's was fortunate to be located close to two railway systems and a branch of the Grand Canal. Therefore the company could forward whiskey to any point on the Grand Canal system or any railway station in Ireland. Its policy was to deliver whiskey 'free on rail or free on canal'.[7]

The continued expansion at the distillery during the 1880s is evident from the increased investment in new plant and machinery. In 1887 Locke's purchased a horizontal cross compound mill engine from the Scottish engineering firm Turnbull, Grant and Jack; the engine was made at the Canal Basin Foundry, Glasgow. The Lockes proudly proclaimed that engine bed and the millstone foundations (which were also installed at this time) were both made with Wexford Cement; this was important to James Harvey who subscribed to the economic nationalist philosophy of buying Irish industrial goods. The installation of the engine enabled the machinery at the distillery to be driven by steam during the summer months when water levels were too low to drive the waterwheel. Therefore the distilling season could be extended.[8] This engine was restored to pristine working order in the mid–1980s. A new set of mash tuns (which still survive) were also purchased from a Scottish company. They bear the stamp mark of 'Bow, Mc Laughlin and Co, Paisley, 1892'. At this stage, Glasgow had become the main centre in the United Kingdom for specialist engineering firms servicing the distilling industry.

Expansion during this period is also clear from the extensive investment in new buildings. To overcome the lack of space in the distillery a large new corn store, kiln and warehouse (now known as Colgan's loft) was built along the west side of the distillery between 1895 and 1897. This was the largest and finest building yet erected in the distillery complex.[9]

At the road end of this large new building, new offices were also built.[10] This was necessary because the whole administrative structure had to be reorganized to cater for the growth in the company's turnover. The volume of book-keeping work had increased so more people were employed in this sphere. Work conditions in the old offices had become cramped and intolerable.

In addition to making major improvements to the machinery and buildings, John Edward and James Harvey also reorganized the company's financial affairs. In 1893 it became incorporated under the companies act. The nominal capital of the new company was £40,000; this was divided into 4000 shares of £10 each. The family held control of all the ordinary shares and John Edward Locke and James Harvey Locke became the new directors. The family, therefore, retained full control of the company. They raised more capital from a public debenture of £25,000, carrying interest at 5 per cent per annum. Part of this was probably used to pay off a bank overdraft which had been used to finance much of the fixed capital investment in new plant and machinery. Apart from the recent installation of the steam engine, the boilers and the mash tuns, other equipment and buildings had been added or improved. Barnard noted in 1886 that the two brothers had 'from time to time made considerable additions to the old work[s] adding new machinery and modern appliances'.[11]

The company's book-keeping methods improved significantly after it became incorporated. It was necessary thereafter to make up an accurate return of the costs and profits made, so the books could be closed on an annual basis and dividends could be payed out to the shareholders. From 1893 onwards a balance sheet was drawn up annually by professional accountants.[12]

Over the years the business had opened accounts with different banks for the purpose of raising capital. Codd and Cuffe in the late 1830s received a cash credit of £3000 from the Moate branch of the National Bank, and they applied to have this raised to £5000. The sum of £3000 was a considerable advance considering that the joint stock of the company was only £3000 in 1833.[13] The Bank of Ireland was much more cautious in their dealings with the distillery. Its agent in Tullamore was permitted by the court of directors in Dublin in 1851 to 'grant a season's credit for £500 to John Locke, upon a deposit of the lease of the head rent of his distillery'. Under the same conditions an advance of £1000 was made in the following year, and in 1854 it was extended to £1500.[14] The distillery subsequently moved its account to the Hibernian Bank in Tullamore. On the company's balance sheet for 1894–5, it appears that Locke's had an overdraft of £4694 with this bank.[15] Seasonal advances from the bank in the autumn and early winter were used to purchase corn. As sales of whiskey brought in cash and cheques, the balance on the account moved back into the black. On a seasonal basis, barley, as the most costly raw material, was always the greatest burden on the company's credit with the banks.

Most of the grain-handling facilities at the distillery were located on the south side of the road. Barnard inspected these maltings, kilns and corn stores on his visit in 1886:

the yard at the back was crowded with farmer's carts, laden with barley put in home-made flax sacks of a primitive shape and nearly 6 feet in length. After inspection by the corn buyer, the barley is hoisted to the different floors and there spread out in to a depth of 3 feet, from whence, as required, it is made to fall through traps on to the malting floors below, each of which possesses a stone steep. The firm make all their own malt, being of the opinion that they can manufacture a finer quality than can be purchased.

Barnard went on to visit the kiln floors which were

both laid with wire cloth and heated by open furnaces. On leaving the kilns, we entered the dry malt stores ... a three storey stone building ... We then proceeded to the raw grain warehouse ... to which is attached a drying corn kiln, floored with worcester perforated tiles which are in great favour among the Irish distillers.[16]

An interesting feature of Locke's grain-handling arrangements was that the grist and malt were stored for a considerable length of time after they had been ground, as this imparted a milder flavour to the whiskey. This required extensive storing facilities since Locke's bought in significant quantities of grain. In the 1891 season, for example, the company bought about 40,000 barrels of corn from local farmers. The importance of good barley for distilling gave the company an incentive to become involved with the

TABLE 8

*Total Cost of Grain and Coal Purchased
Per Annum at Lockes, 1894–1900 (to nearest pound)*

	COAL	GRAIN
1894–5	£1468	£8917
1895–6	£1478	£10188
1896–7	£1477	£9444
1897–8	£1484	£9386
1898–9	£1602	£8096
1899–1900	£1865	£8604

Source: National Library, Ms 20011, Private Ledger, 1895–1900.

TABLE 9
Labourers' Wages at Lockes, 1873–1934 (6-day week)

	WAGES	SAUERBECK PRICE INDEX (1867–77=100)	AVERAGE PRICE BREAD DUBLIN (PENCE PER 4 LB)
1873	10s	111	8.5
1876	10s	95	7.5
1879	8s	83	7.5
1882	9s	84	7.5
1885	9s	72	6
1888	9s	70	6.5
1891	9s	72	6.5
1894	9s	63	5
1897	9s	62	5.5
1900	9s	75	5.5
1903	9s	69	5.5
1906	9s-10s	77	5.5
1910	10s	78	6.5
1913	10s	85	6
1916	13s	136	9.5
1919	£1 5s–£1 7s	206	10
1922	£1 15s–£1.17s	131	11
1925	£1 12s	136	11
1928	£1 10s	120	10.5
1931	£1 10s	83	8.5
1934	£1 10s	82	9
1936	£1 10s	89	9.5
1939	£1 10s	94	10.5
1942	£1 15s		12
1945	£2 6s		13.5
1952	£4 2s–£4 19s		

Sources: National Library; Ms 20051–60 Workmen's Accounts; B.R. Mitchell, *British Historical Statistics* (1988), pp. 725, 771.

Seed Barley Association, whose aim was to improve the crop. Locke's became distributors of seed and gave information to local farmers on how they could improve their barley. For preparing the grain, there were two mills operating at the distillery; one with four pairs of stones for grinding malt and barley, and another with two pairs for

Two views of
Locke's Distillery
and a third of the
market-place in
Kilbeggan, Co.
Westmeath, taken
from the original
glass-plate photo-
graphs of William
Lawrence during
the 1890s.

Mary Anne Locke (*née* Devereux), who established the Convent of Mercy in Kilbeggan in 1879.

John Edward Locke, *c.* 1915. (Family photographs are by courtesy of Patricia Tinney.)

James Harvey and Florence Locke (right) with Dick Coffey (left), *c.* 1900.

'The Mahout at the meet': Mary Locke, commandant of the Bloomfield Red Cross Hospital, with Lieutenant-General Sir Bryan Mahon, former G.O.C. troops in Ireland, out for a day's sport in Westmeath, *c.* 1920.

Sweetie Locke with dogs Whisper (left), and Wankie and Winkey (above).

1757

IRISH

POT STILL WHISKEY

DISTILLED BY

John Locke & Co. Ltd.

Ireland's Oldest Distillers

BOTTLED BY THE VENDOR

10 YEARS OLD

DISTILLED BY
John Locke &
PURE
POT STILL
Whiskey

ESTABLISHED 1757

KILBEGGAN
IRELAND.

Locke's

SINGLE MALT

BRUSNA DISTILLERY

PURE POT STILL

Irish Whiskey

John Locke & Co. Ltd

ESTABLISHED 1757

DISTILLED MATURED AND BOTTLED IN IRELAND
BY JOHN LOCKE & CO. KILBEGGAN IRELAND

N° JL 001
of 5000

70 cl   PRODUCT OF IRELAND   40% vol

70° PROOF

ESTD
1757

Locke's
REGISTERED TRADE MARK
Liqueur
Whiskey

Distilled & Matured at
BRUSNA DISTILLERY

Makers of Finest Whiskey
for 200 Years

PRODUCE OF REPUBLIC

IRELAND

LOCKE'S KILBEGGAN WHISKEY.
GUARANTEED
PURE POT STILL

BOTTLED BY P & H. EGAN, Ltd., Tullamore,

AND AT MOYVORE, BALLYCUMBER, KILCORMAC, RATHANGAN

ESTABLISHED 1757

THE OLDEST DISTILLERY IN IRELAND

John Locke & Co., Ltd.
Kilbeggan.

Distillers of Pure
Pot Still
Whiskey

Dear Sir (or Madam),

We beg to call your attention to the temporary easing of the supply position of whiskey, which is due to various causes. In view of the approach of the summer tourist season this easing of supply is unlikely to continue long, and consumers are urged to replenish their stocks while they can get supplies.

We respectfully suggest that you should place your future orders as soon as possible with your usual wholesaler, or, if you prefer, direct with the Distillery.

For the latter purpose, we append an order form showing our current prices.

Yours faithfully,

John Locke & Company Limited.

ORDER FORM

Please forward to me :—

A............Gallons in bulk @ 161/- per gallon   ...   .   £

B............Cases of Old Kilbeggan whiskey in Bottles @ 336/6 per case £

C............Cases of Old Kilbegan whiskey in Pints @ 507/- per case (3 galls) £

D............Cases of Old Kilbeggan whiskey in ½ – Pints @ 343/6 per case £

E........ Cases of Old Kilbeggan whiskey in Naggins @ 352/- per case £

F............Cases of Old Kilbeggan whiskey in Babies @ 357/6 per case £

TOTAL

Cases 10/- extra (returnable).

Jars £2 extra (returnable).

NAME..

ADDRESS...

COUNTY..

The McCormack family: Count John (left), Gwen, Lily and Cyril (right), who was to marry Patricia Locke and work for the distillery in the 1950s.

The 'T-Siphon' warehouse under construction during 1949, designed by a young Trinity graduate after a building in the ancient Iraqi city of Ure.

The great mill-stones, used to grind malted barley for the mash.

A cooper at work on the 40-gallon oaken casks in the distillery yard.

Locke's today, with its water-wheel and mill-race above the river Brosna.

grinding oatmeal.[17] Locke's sold their 'patent oatmeal' until the 1880s when it was discontinued because of the need for more space in the distillery as output was increasing. But oatmeal continued to be ground for mashing purposes.[18]

Barley, oats, rye and wheat were delivered to the distillery door by local farmers. This gave Locke's certain cost advantages over its larger rivals located in Dublin, who either had to pay large sums to transport corn from the Irish countryside or import it. Locke's, however, had higher costs for coal.

Coal was imported from Welsh or Scottish collieries. This was shipped to Dublin and from there taken by canal to Kilbeggan. A small amount of coal also came from the colliery at Castlecomer in Co. Kilkenny.[19] Supplies for the cooperage also came via rail or canal from Dublin.[20] The company held shares in both the Grand Canal Company and the Great Southern and Western Railway,[21] which may have entitled the distillery to special freight rates with these companies.

Employment at the distillery rose between the 1860s and the 1880s, as output increased. In the 1873–4 season, about 42 people were employed at the distillery between the months of November and April (see table 5, p. 47). Barnard noted that about 70 people were employed when he visited the distillery in 1886. When trade was very good, as in 1883, up to 120 hands were employed (presumably including clerical staff). When the distilling season finished, employment dropped dramatically; many employees were given work on the various farms run by the Lockes, notably at Ardnaglue and Ballard.[22] The seasonal upswing in the demand for agricultural labour coincided with the slack period at the distillery. During this time of year some of the distillery workers became involved in turf-cutting. A skeleton staff of clerical workers, storemen and whatever craftsmen were required to carry out repairs and maintenance were kept on at the distillery during the slack period.

The price of labour at Locke's distillery remained remarkably stable from the 1880s to 1906. Inflation rose sharply over the following decades and wages also rose. Relative to the cost of bread, wages improved considerably: they were four times higher in 1945 than they had been in 1873, while bread had not even doubled in price. Judging by the Sauerbeck price index, the purchasing power of labour increased significantly over the decade and a half after the First World War, but employment at Locke's was considerably down during this period, which was a major time of recession for the distilling industry.

Despite the installation of the most up-to-date plant and equipment at Locke's between the 1870s and the 1890s, the distilling techniques remained quite old-fashioned. In contrast to the advances in engineering, there seemed to be little knowledge filtering through from the sciences into the process of distilling at Kilbeggan. Instead, a reverence for the rule-of-thumb methods which had been passed down from generation to generation persisted; these had evolved through trial and error rather than through any rational application of scientific knowledge. Certain old vessels were retained despite the modernization of the plant; according to Barnard, Locke's used the same method of distillation which was used when the distillery was established.[23]

In 1949, when J.J. Hogan arrived at Locke's to take up a job as a distiller, many old-fashioned methods were still being used. Wort and wash, for example, were being pumped around in open troughs so that mould, wild yeast and mill dust could get into the liquid.[24] The course of fermentation could therefore be unpredictable. This lack of uniformity would have affected the character of the whiskey, which must have varied significantly from period to period.

An interesting account of the distillery was featured in the *King's County Chronicle* on 16 of August 1883. This passage casts some light on the appearance and structure of the distillery at this time:

Splendidly situated on the banks of the Brusna, the handsome residence of Mr John Locke and the enormous pile of buildings forming the distillery, mills, malt houses, stores, etc present an imposing appearance. On the left hand side as you enter from Tullamore are Mr Locke's residence, beautiful garden, spacious yard and stables, as well as malt houses, kilns and corn stores, and on the right are the distillery, the mills and warehouses ... The malt houses have a capacity for steeping at one time 200 barrels of barley, while the kilns attached are capable of drying the same quantity at one cast. There are also two kilns for drying raw corn, which are capable of containing 180 barrels at a time. The establishment has storage for 15,000 barrels of barley, 2000 barrels of oats, and 4000 barrels of malt. In case of a press of business the corn kilns could dry 800 barrels in 24 hours. There are two immense warehouses. No. 1 is 136 feet by 40 feet, and capable of storing 3000 casks of whiskey. No. 2 is 180 feet by 150 feet and can contain 6000 casks. There are two mills – one with four pairs of stones for grinding malt and barley and the other with two pairs for grinding oatmeal for mashing purposes. As there is a never failing supply from the Brusna, water is the only power employed in working the machinery, which is driven by two large wheels, whose combined action may be estimated at 50 horse power.

In order to produce a whiskey of mild flavour, Messrs Locke always leave the malt and grain stored for a considerable time after being ground before they use them for mashing. This is the plan adopted by the most eminent distillers. The cleansing arrangements on the premises are of the most perfect order so that the slightest supervision of the manager over the different vessels used for brewing and fermenting purposes is sufficient to show him whether they are in a satisfactory state. Steam is used for heating the brewing tanks, and the machinery for mashing is so complete that in this department no hitch occurs from one end of the season to the other. The mashing tuns are capable of running off from the first brewing 14,000 gallons of strong worts for the fermenting backs and the wort is cooled by pipes laid in the head race of No. 2 waterwheel, and afterwards into No. 2 underback. To get the uniform temperature for fermenting purposes a supply from No. 1 underback can always be had. From an appliance fixed to the discharge pipes of the mash tuns a clear wort is always ensured, which is most necessary for perfect fermentation. The cooling pipes are on the same plan as refrigerators but from their being much larger and having a far greater supply of water from their situation at the head race they can cool a far larger quantity of wort in the same time. When the wort is reduced to the proper temperature it is put into the fermenting backs, of which Messrs Locke have nine capable of holding 14,000 gallons, in addition to these a wash charger of the same size is utilized during the period for holding the fermented wash and the back from which this has been taken is then refitted. I understand that in the distillery the attenuation of the wash can always be favourably compared with that of any other ... which is an important consideration in extracting the full quantity of spirit. There are four stills in the establishment, two of which are capable of holding at one time 30,000 gallons of wash between them, and the other two (low wine stills) contain 8000 gallons each. From the peculiar formation of the worms their distillations are always very clean and the mixtures used by Messrs Locke are those of the most eminent distillery in Dublin. The distilling department is capable of turning out 300,000 gallons per season. The trade of Messrs Locke, though extensive in England, is done principally in Ireland, as they can obtain higher prices here. During the season about 120 hands are employed at the distillery, and at its termination most of these men are retained to work on the farm. Messrs Locke are very liberal towards their employees as they invariably support the widows of men who die in their employment. Mr Walter Furlong, a gentleman of long experience and well known ability, is the present manager of the distillery.

Furlong, the manager, worked for the Lockes for many years. The family respected his knowledge of the distilling process and the structure of the business. When Locke's became a limited liability company in 1893, Walter Furlong was made one of the three directors of the company.[24] This was a mark of the Locke's respect for him and an acknowledgement of his services to the company.

When not engaged in running the distillery, the Lockes spent much of their leisure time riding horses. James Harvey began hunting at the tender age of seven and he indulged in this sport for the rest of his life. On a number of occasions the Tullamore Harriers would stop for lunch at Ardnaglue, after chasing a hare or fox all morning across the countryside on the borders of Westmeath and King's County (Offaly). For many years James Harvey kept his own pack of harriers. Although he spent much time running the distillery, he also had time for country pursuits. When his mother moved to Ardnaglue in the early 1870s, James Harvey was in his early teens. Thereafter, he remained at Ardnaglue, which effectively became his country seat after the death of his mother in 1889. Since he never took on the responsibilities of family life he could devote his spare time to leading the full life of a country gentleman. James Harvey also took care of the family's farming interests, so he probably also socialized with some of the local landlords and larger farmers in the area.[25]

Apart from hunting he rode at point-to-points and played polo. Racing was one of his great joys. As a young man he kept a large racing establishment at the Curragh. A number of prestigious races were won in his colours, and he personally rode a number of winners at Kilbeggan. He held large parties at Ardnaglue and was extremely popular in all parts of the county. In the Westmeath Polo Club Races, for example, at Ledeston in 1888, he had a winning streak: 'Mr J.H. Locke's three wins were received with hearty enthusiasm, clearly showing the popularity in which that gentleman (who hails from Kilbeggan) is held about here.'[26]

John Cantwell of Kilbeggan (aged ninety-six when interviewed) clearly remembers 'Jimmy Locke' (as he was known locally) at the races in Kilbeggan when he was an old man. John remembered him clearing the course for each race. James Harvey did not race very often at this stage, but on this occasion he had a challenge race of three miles with another man. James Harvey had a black horse called Sweet, who unfortunately was much older than the challenger's horse. All went well for James Harvey until the third round when Sweet ran into a large marshy ditch. John Cantwell recounted how he pulled James Harvey out of this ditch, and on finishing the story he noted that 'Jimmy had always been a great sport.' James Harvey certainly must have cut a dash on a horse since he was fine tall man of 6 ft 4 in. in height. His brother John was tall, too, but much plumper. The Lockes also opened a cricket club in Kilbeggan. Their adoption of this most English of games is another example of the Lockes' pursuit of respectability. The team was probably drawn from the local gentry and the town's Catholic middle class. The club was also used for a range of other social activities.

During the era of Parnell, Father Brogan's band prac-

tised in the cricket club. This band had been set up early in
1891 as a focus for the anti-Parnellite faction in Kilbeggan.
It was a stormy period when allegiances were strongly divided. Initially the Lockes appear to have been on the side
of Parnell. They lent their horse-drawn carriage to the Kilbeggan Parnellites so that they could attend a meeting in
Mullingar in May 1891. *The Westmeath Nationalist*, which
was rabidly anti-Parnell, expressed reservations about this:

Tis a matter of surprise that the deservedly popular owners of the Brusna
Distillery should take sides on this occasion. We expected otherwise,
seeing they were always with the people. Without any signs of approval
save their leader's own 'magnificent flash of silence,' the Parnellites
moved peacefully away. All the Parnellites of Kilbeggan – a miserable
handful – attended the meeting, even the children.

During the day we were compensated for the absence of our friends
by the music, so excellently rendered, of the new band started under the
presidency of the Rev. Father Brogan.

What has become of the Kilbeggan band? Why did they not play the
Parnellites out of town?

The stillness of the evening was disturbed soon by the stentorian
tones of the 'Bishop' calling out 'to h—l with Parnell.' Two only of the
employees of Messrs Locke, numbering about seventy, went to the
meeting – Mark Hope and the Doctor.'

Under this kind of pressure from the Church, which
effectively mobilized Kilbeggan against Parnell, the Lockes
soon changed their position. They made available the cricket ground pavilion for Father Brogan's band and provided
hospitality to members of the band on a number of occasions, much to the delight of *The Westmeath Nationalist*
which made this known. It was obviously important in any
issue in Kilbeggan to have the Lockes on one's side.[27]

The popularity of James Harvey and his social position in
the town made him an obvious candidate for local politics.
In 1899 he stood as a candidate in the election for the
Westmeath County Council. The following appeared in the
Westmeath Examiner on the eve of the election:

WESTMEATH COUNTY COUNCIL
TO THE ELECTORS OF THE KILBEGGAN DISTRICT

Ladies and Gentlemen,

I am desirous of becoming your representative for this district on the County Council, and I believe that the long connection of my business with your interests, to our mutual advantage, entice me to look forward with confidence to your support.

So far I have taken little or no part in politics, and your interests would be my only consideration in any matter that would come before the Council.

I have spent the whole of my life among you; many of you are in my employment, and I consider the election of a representative unconnected with the manufacturing interest of Kilbeggan would be very undesirable. I am in favour not only of a Catholic University, but also of Technical Education, as tending to qualify the people for skilled labour by enlarging the manufacturing possibilities of our country.

I am strongly in favour that the surplus duties – amounting to about £120,000 a year in Ireland – accruing from the Wine, Spirit and Beer Duties Act of 1800, should be handed to the local authorities, as is done in Great Britain, for expenditure on Technical Education, or otherwise, as they think fit.

I am also of opinion that those rates that have of necessity to be paid, be, as far as possible, expended for the benefit of the labouring classes in the districts paying those rates; and I can promise you, if entrusted to my care, your interests shall be safeguarded to the best of my ability.

Yours faithfully,

JAMES H. LOCKE
Ardnaglue, Kilbeggan.[28]

James Harvey was duly elected to the Kilbeggan Rural District Council. Over the next years he supported the development of Irish industrial resources by advocating the use of articles like Irish cement and slates instead of those imported from Britain. He seems to have been a reasonably progressive member of the council in the face of strong opposition. In 1907, for example, he supported the county surveyor's suggestion that the road between Tyrrellspass and Horseleap and the streets of Kilbeggan should be steam-rolled; although this was more expensive than using direct labour in the short term, it lasted longer. Most of the council members objected to the proposal on cost grounds. James Harvey pointed out that he had come back from Radnorshire in Wales, which is a small, poorer place than this, and the roads are all steam rolled. In the North of Ireland where I have the most of my business to do the roads are all steam rolled. I am one of the largest rate payers in the district and employers of labour, and I consider that we should give it a trial.

But his more progressive approach was rejected out of hand and the proposal was thrown out.[29]

The influence of the Church on the Locke family remained strong. There was a private chapel in Brusna House, and the family maintained its strong link with the Sisters of Mercy in the town. John Edward's daughters subsequently laid the foundation-stone for the main buildings of the convent, and employees and horses from the distillery drew the stones to build it. Even in the years before the distillery closed, employees sometimes helped out with maintenance and repair work at the convent. But at times the links between the family and the sisters became somewhat strained. The marriages and living arrangements of James Harvey and John Edward were not always strictly in line with the conventional teachings of the Catholic Church. Their high social status, however, enabled them to thwart the Church's position on marriage. James Harvey never got married, but he had a mistress called Florence Savage for whom he built a small cottage close to Ardnaglue (the Glebe). The relationship was a fairly long-standing one and his commitment to her can be seen from the fact that on his death Florence was left Ardnaglue, in addition to receiving by far the largest legacy in his will. Florence had previously been married and had a child who died at a young age. Her maiden name was Edwards and she met James Harvey through the relationship which developed between his brother and her sister Mary. The father of Mary and Florence was one of the chief engineers who worked under Dargan in the construction of much of the Irish railway network. The large family which they grew up in, therefore, moved around Ireland so that Mr Edwards was sufficiently close to the ever-shifting location of his work. Unfortunately, Edwards died in an accident while at work on the railways near Mullingar. His wife was left with at least ten children and no money.[30]

In 1880 John Locke married Mary Edwards. She was married off to him when she was only seventeen years of age as her mother was eager to ease the burden of her large family. Mary was as enthusiastic about hunting as her brother-in-law, James Harvey. Her gregarious disposition was probably a result of growing up within such a large family. She affectionately became known as 'Muds' within the Locke family. After her marriage to John Edward, the couple moved into Brusna House. In August 1882, they had their first child who was christened Mary Evelyn (Sweet). A second child, Florence Emily (Flo), was born a few years later. But the marriage was not a happy one. Mary had a number of affairs with various gentlemen in the area, much to the chagrin of John Edward, who forced her to leave Brusna House in 1895.[31]

John Edward subsequently sued for divorce and a settlement was reached at the Probate and Matrimonial Court in Dublin in February 1896. Only Kitty O'Shea's divorce had attracted as much attention in Kilbeggan. According to a newspaper report the court was very crowded:

An extra policeman was placed at the door to prevent any overcrowding, but a goodly number succeeded in securing places. Mr Locke sat beside his council, and was apparently in a dejected mood, resting his chin upon his right hand, while Mrs Locke, her sister and friends sat near the witness box. Mrs Locke was evidently as much affected as her husband, but her sisters and friends were observed to be in a rather cheerful mood. They smiled and engaged in conversations that provoked slight laughter among themselves. The respondent invariably cast furtive glances at her husband, who did not even once, after taking his seat in court, look in her direction.[32]

A settlement was reached by both parties, predominantly in the interests of the children, and further litigation and public embarrassment was thereby avoided.

Mary and the children moved into a fine house near Kilbeggan called Ballinagore. They received an allowance of £600 per annum from John Edward, which is what she had received from him for the household expenses prior to their marriage break-up. One of the points he made during the divorce proceedings was that little of this money was being spent on the household. This award provides some idea of John Edwards income which must have been well over £1200 per annum. This would indicate that the income of the Lockes was much greater than that of most successful lawyers and other professionals. Despite this wealth, Mary had obviously not been altogether satisfied with the life of a housewife. She continued living the sporting life after moving to Ballinagore, following the Westmeath hounds over every terrain. Her two daughters, Sweet and Flo, both grew up to be accomplished riders in the Westmeath hunt, and also rode in many point to points.[33]

'Muds' Locke was one of the first women to drive a car in Westmeath, which is an interesting indication of her social status. There is a story in the family that on one occasion she ran over a policeman's toe on Sackville St (now O'Connell St) in Dublin; leaning out of the car window she suggested to him that he should take his toes out of the way the next time. 'Muds' was always eager to inform people of her elevated social status. One of her granddaughters remembered always being embarrassed when accompanying her into Dublin's foremost department stores where she would announce in a loud voice, 'I'm Mrs Locke.' 'Muds' was somewhat angered when shop assistants did not appreciate the significance of this.

During the First World War she became actively involved in the Red Cross, spending some time working in hospitals in France. She received medals from the French government for her efforts. Before the end of the war she returned to help out in the Westmeath Auxiliary Red Cross Hospital in Mullingar, where she became the Commandant. It is interesting to note the significant contribution of the Locke family and their in-laws towards the British war effort. Sweet and Flo both married men who fought in the British army during the war. In a political context, their situation was probably not untypical of many members of the Catholic middle class. Republicanism was still a fringe ideology in 1914, and when Redmond announced that support for the British war effort was the best way to copper-fasten Home Rule, many Irish Catholics answered the call.

John Edward remained at Brusna House as a single man after the departure of his wife and family. His housekeeper, Mary Cranley, also lived in the house.[34] The portrait of John Edward painted in his later years (which now hangs in the distillery office) gives the impression that he was not a happy man; his face portrays a certain degree of bitterness. His broken marriage obviously weighed heavily on him, he did not have the same appetite for life as his brother. Kit Carney remembered his father, who worked for the Lockes, telling him that he had been sent out to fetch John Edwards' Christmas dinner in 1900: two salted herrings, which he ate alone. But his stoic nature was in no way harmful to his management of the affairs of the distillery just across the road from his house. He was available at all hours for duty in this respect. James Harvey, in contrast, was far enough out of town to avoid these intrusions on his social life.

The incorporation of the distillery in 1893 was initially reasonably successful for the Lockes. The company paid a dividend of 10 per cent in 1895 and 1896, rising to 15 per cent in 1897. However, this was reduced to 12.6 per cent in 1899, possibly because the fortunes of the industry were being affected by the over-supply of whiskey on the market.[35] The major development within the industry during the last quarter of the nineteenth century was the growth of patent still production. The Irish pot still producers were already suffering from a glut on the market by the turn of the century. At this stage patent still whiskey accounted for 72 per cent of the whiskey produced in Ireland. In the face of this competition pot still producers, like

Locke's, were finding that the market for their product was severely curtailed. Pot still production in Ireland was cut back from 6.079 million proof gallons in 1890 to 4.136 million proof gallons in 1900.[36]

The decline in sales was not the only problem Locke's had during these years. Around 1901 a paraffin lamp exploded in the lower mill and a fire broke out which consumed everything except the stone walls. The buildings were reconstructed, though the marks of the fire can still be seen on the stonework of the lower mill. But trade was so bad until the war years that it was not until 1918 that the mill machinery was overhauled and brought back into use by Messrs Henry Simon of Stockport.[37]

Locke's sales diminished considerably between 1890 and 1910. In 1886 sales were in the region of 150,000 gallons; by the 1908–9 season they had fallen to about 50,000 gallons. Exports in that year accounted for about 11,500 gallons, most of this going to Britain (and about 600 gallons to the USA). The major change which had taken place was that Locke's had lost its large trade with Dublin; less than 100 gallons went to the city in that year. In contrast, Belfast, which had been an unimportant destination for Locke's sales in 1869–70, took almost 18,000 gallons during the 1908–9 season.[38] The bulk of the consignments to Belfast would have been purchased by the blenders of that city, who at this stage dominated the Irish whiskey trade, because they controlled the Irish share of the British market for blended whiskey. Dublin's dogmatic determination to stick with pot still production ignored consumer preference in Britain. During the last third of the nineteenth century Dublin, therefore, lost its traditional domination of the Irish distilling industry to Belfast, a city which now completely dominated the Irish industrial sector.

It is possible to make a comparison of the geographical distribution of the company's sales in 1861–2 and 1908–9 from surviving Sales Day Books (see table 10). These figures are based on the number of sales, so they do not indi-

TABLE 10
A Comparison of the Destinations of Locke's Sales in
1861–2 and 1908–9 (number of individual orders)

	1861–2	1908–9
Westmeath	269	200
Offaly	48	38
Roscommon	43	22
Dublin	37	19
Galway	8	36
Kildare	6	7
Cork		43
Mayo		30
Limerick		30
Tyrone		3
Sligo		16
Waterford		19
Tipperary		14
Belfast		41
Armagh		8
Leitrim		11
Louth		1
Antrim		1
Cavan		5
Longford		14
Kerry		1
Clare		7
Londonderry		8
Carlow		1
Britain	2	66
Germany		5
USA		6
TOTALS	414	647

Source: National Library, Ms 20020 and 20021, Sales Books.

cate how significant the quantity of whiskey sold to Belfast
blenders had become (i.e. it does not distinguish between
large sales and small sales). But they demonstrate how
Locke's market had become more widely dispersed geographically.

Locke's output had fallen back by 1908-9 to the same level as in the late 1860s. Employment levels had also decreased to the numbers employed in the 1870s. There were only 44 people on the wage list at the beginning of December 1914. The outbreak of the First World War brought an improvement in the distillery's fortunes. War always led to a rise in the consumption of whiskey, and restrictions were usually imposed on distillers using corn and coal, so existing stocks of whiskey rose in terms of both demand and value.[39] Although we have no output figures for this period we can assume that output at Locke's followed a reasonably similar trajectory as at the neighbouring distillery at Tullamore. In Tullamore output rose from 50,000 proof gallons in 1910 to 100,000 proof gallons in 1916. In 1919 and 1920 it jumped to over 200,000 proof gallons, dropping back dramatically to only 20,000 proof gallons in 1924.[40]

The export trade to Britain was important during the war years. Locke's was also trying to open up new markets in the USA. Some surviving correspondence to Jennings, a New York spirit dealer and importer, indicates that a small trade had slowly been built up with New York since the turn of the century.[41] But the introduction of Prohibition in the USA in January 1920, closed off a market which was beginning to show some promise. The buoyant trade during and after the war years also came to an abrupt end for Locke's around this time; in the early 1920s production at the distillery ceased for a short period.[42] Exports to Britain remained important for Locke's and indeed for the whole industry as consumption on the home market had almost collapsed. Between 1924 and 1926 exports accounted for over 40 per cent of the total sales of whiskey in the 26 counties (see table 11, p. 79).

The beginning of the 1920s marked something of a turning-point in the distillery's fortunes. Thereafter, the state of the company further deteriorated. Ominously, during the first month of the 1920s John Edward Locke died.[43] The management of the distillery for some time prior to his death seems to have passed largely into the hands of his younger brother, James Harvey. Upon his death John Edward, possessed 1136 ordinary shares in the company and 139 debentures.[44] James Harvey at this stage possessed 2013 of the 4000 shares in the company. The remaining shares were held by members of the Locke family or the husbands of John Edward's daughters, with the exception of a mere 200 shares which were in the possession of the company's bank manager in Tullamore, and Thomas Coffey, the chief distiller. John Edward's wife, Mary (who lived on into the 1940s), still held 769 shares in 1921 and her daughters, Mary Evelyn and Florence Emily owned 384 each.[45]

James Harvey lived for only a few more years, dying in November 1927. The editor of the *Offaly Independent* wrote in his obituary that the firm was 'carried on with marked success in former years affording employment to about 70 hands. [it was] due to him that the name of the firm is known far and wide'. It added that 'present day conditions have seriously affected output'.[46] Consumption of whiskey in Ireland at this point was at an all time low, as were the fortunes of the company. Production had been suspended in 1924 and distilling was not resumed until 1931.[47] The bleak years continued after James Harvey's death. The two brothers had seen the distillery through its best years in the 1880s, but their deaths came at a time when the distillery was experiencing a major crisis. By 1919 patent still whiskey produced 81 per cent of total output in Ireland, and the diminishing share of the market which pot still producers could command slowly squeezed the sales of distillers like Locke's.[48]

NOTES

1. W. Coyne, *Ireland, Industrial and Agricultural* (Dublin 1902), p. 502.
2. E.B. Maguire, *Irish Whiskey* (Dublin 1973), p.3.
3. L. Cullen, *An Economic History of Ireland Since 1660* (London

1972), p. 158.
4. Maguire, p. 274.
5. National Library, Locke's Tribunal, Cooney's evidence, Q. 1068.
6. National Library, Ms 20041, re-dip book, 1894–1909; Warehouse Book 1900–11; Racking book, 1890–1937 (both kept at Kilbeggan in the possession of Brian Quinn); exports calculated from Ms 20020, Sales Day Book, 1861–71.
7. *Westmeath Examiner*, 6 January 1906; Cullen, p. 145. Warehouse books 1911–38, 1939–56 (kept in Kilbeggan in Brian Quinn's possession).
8. J. Bailey, 'New Life at 100', *Stationary Engine Research Group Bulletin*, 1989, vol. 11, no. 4; *Westmeath Examiner*, 30 March 1907.
9. National Library, Ms 20011, Private Ledger, 1895–1909.
10. *Ibid.*
11. A. Barnard, *The Whiskey Distilleries of the UK* (London 1887), p. 393.
12. S. Pollard, *The Genesis of Modern Management* (1965), p. 216, See Appendix 2 and 3.
13. Registry of Deeds, Dublin, Codd to Reynolds, Book 22, 202, 6 December 1839; Memorial, Brett, Codd, Cuffe, Book 12, no. 86, 1833.
14. Bank of Ireland, Head Office, Baggot Street, Court of Directors Transactions, no. 18, 2 December 1851, 28 September 1852, 7 November 1854.
15. National Library, Ms 20011, Private Ledger, 1895–1909; Ms 20069, Hibernian Bank Pass Book, 1905–1920.
16. Barnard, p. 393.
17. *King's County Chronicle*, 16 August 1883; *Westmeath Nationalist*, 22 October 1891,*Westmeath Examiner*, 26 March 1887.
18. Barnard, p. 394.
19. National Library, Ms 20011, Private Ledger, 1895–1909; Coal Book, 1917–57 (in possession of Brian Quinn, Kilbeggan).
20. National Library, Ms 20062, Miscellaneous Ledger, 1858–71.
21. National Library, Ms 20088, Miscellaneous Statistics, 1886–1951; Ms 20011, Private Ledger, 1895–1909.
22. *King's County Chronicle*, 16 August 1883; Barnard, p. 394; *The Westmeath Nationalist*, 22 October 1891.
23. Barnard, p. 394.
24. General Entry Book, 1867–1913.
25. *Westmeath Examiner*, 25 February 1899, 16 August 1958; *Offaly Independent*, 19 November 1927.
26. *Westmeath Examiner*, 21 July 1888, 21 October 1899, 22 September 1900, 2 May 1903. James Harvey helped to revive the Kilbeggan Races at Loughnagore around 1900, the annual event had been

discontinued for a number of years.

27. *Westmeath Nationalist*, 14 May 1891, 6 August 1891, 24 September 1891, 14 January 1892.
28. *Westmeath Examiner*, 25 February 1899.
29. *Ibid.*, 30 March 1907.
30. Copy of James Harvey Locke's Will and Codicil, in possession of Brian Quinn, Kilbeggan. I would like to thank Mrs Morgan (granddaughter of John Locke) for information on Florence and Mary Edwards, and the Dargan connection.
31. *Westmeath Independent*, 25 January 1896.
32. *Ibid.*, 25 January 1896, 29 February 1896.
33. I would like to thank Mrs Tish Tinny who provided some information on the family. She also kindly lent me some family photograph albums, put together by her grandmother, which contain newspaper cuttings, much information has been used from these in the following paragraphs.
34. *Westmeath Examiner*, 16 August 1958; National Archives, Census Returns 1901, Kilbeggan.
35. National Library, Ms 20011, Private Ledger, 1895–1909.
36. R. Weir, 'In and Out of Ireland, The Distillers Company Limited and the Irish Whiskey Trade', *Irish Social and Economic History Journal*, vol. 7, pp. 46–53.
37. National Library, Ms 20100(14), Locke to Simon, 7 December 1954; Folklore Commission Archive, UCD, School Collection 1937-8, vol. 733, pp. 52–4.
38. National Library, Ms 20021, Sales Day Book.
39. National Library, Workmen's Accounts, Ms 20072(6), Memorandum with the Transport and General Workers' Union.
40. Byrne, p. 226.
41. Telegram 19 January; letters between Locke and Jennings 18 January, 2 February, 8 & 10 March, 4 & 28 March, 4 & 28 April, 19 May, 6 June 1916 (in possession of Brian Quinn).
42. National Library, Ms 20072(6), *op cit.*
43. *Freeman's Journal*, 2 February 1920; *Westmeath Examiner*, 7 February 1920.
44. National Archives, Dublin, Will of John Edward Locke (died 1920).
45. Companies' Registration Office, Dublin, D. 1610, no. 2, December 1921.
46. *Offaly Independent*, 19 November 1927.
47. National Library, Ms 20072(6), op cit.
48. Weir, *op cit.* and also 'The Patent Still Distillers and the Role of Competition', in L. Cullen and T. Smout (eds), *Scottish and Irish Economic and Social History 1600–1900* (Edinburgh 1977), p. 138.

6

DEPRESSION, WAR AND SCANDAL
1927–1948

The consumption of spirits in Ireland continued to follow a downward trajectory during the 1920s and early 1930s. Distilleries like Locke's, which produced only pot still whiskey, were particularly badly hit by this drop in demand. In addition, the export market to Britain declined during this period. The Scotch industry was also suffering from a severe contraction of demand on the British market. Scotch exports to the USA were effectively terminated by the introduction in 1920 of Prohibition, which was to continue until 1933. Although very little Irish whiskey was exported to the USA, the curtailment of the Scotch trade in that market made it all the more difficult for Irish whiskey to sell in an over-supplied British market. The Scotch trade in potable whiskey did not start to recover until the mid-1930s.[1]

As a consequence of this major downturn, distilling at Locke's was suspended between 1924 and 1931, and there was a dramatic deterioration in the company's finances. In order to prevent a forced liquidation during these years James Harvey's shares (2013 out of a total of 4000) were transferred in 1928 to the Hibernian Bank in Dublin as security for the company's growing liabilities. The financial problems experienced by Locke's were by no means unique, this depression fell heavily on the industry at large. Three of the seven distilleries in the 26 counties closed in 1924; Kilbeggan was the only one of these which reopened. Most of the workforce was laid off during these years, which caused great hardship in the town. The *West-*

TABLE 11
Spirits Released from Bond in Ireland (26 counties) for Home Consumption and Export (proof gallons)

YEAR	HOME CONSUMPTION	EXPORT	TOTAL
1924	884,179	578,475	1,462,654
1925	751,867	1,012,083	1,763,950
1926	656,887	457,691	457,691
1927	663,469	207,189	870,658
1928	642,361	203,341	845,602
1929	663,770	197,934	861,704
1930	635,243	194,583	829,826
1931	608,581	164,241	772,822
1932	577,077	123,039	700,116
1933	542,013	110,452	652,465
1934	490,956	265,551	756,507
1935	469,621	127,775	497,396
1936	482,659	190,758	673,417
1937	499,475	289,347	788,822
1938	494,769	226,359	721,128
1939	494,242	167,239	661,481
1940	479,824	253,208	733,032
1941	454,789	330,392	785,181
1942	503,998	805,986	1,309,584
1943	520,233	209,834	730,067
1944	546,845	153,250	700,095
1945	596,242	108,040	704,282
1946	651,190	467,708	1,118,898
1947	631,521	273,333	904,854
1948	656,685	307,823	964,508
1949	697,903	400,323	1,368,226
1950	747,719	427,832	1,175,551
1951	786,734	414,627	1,201,361
1952	770,297	458,784	1,229,081
1953	565,866	304,755	870,621

Sources: National Archives, Irish Distillers Collection, Irish Pot Still Distillers Association, 1955.

meath Examiner reported in October 1928 that because of the lack of employment at the distillery, more people than usual were on the list of the St Vincent de Paul Society. When distilling was finally resumed on a small scale in 1931, the outlook for the industry remained bleak; world depression and the high duty on spirits led to sluggish sales for most of the 1930s. Confidence in the industry was therefore at a low ebb.[2]

Exports of whiskey and the quantity released from bond for home consumption continued to fall between 1924 and 1939. The figures in table 11 show the continuing contraction of the industry, which had begun before the end of the nineteenth century in the south of Ireland. There had been 19 distilleries in the 26 counties in 1893, by 1931 there were only 5 left; Locke's, Tullamore, Power's, Jameson and Cork Distillers' Co.[3] Drinking habits were changing in Ireland. While there is little doubt that society was beginning to attach greater importance to sobriety, the major rise in the duty on spirits between 1909 and 1952 must also have contributed significantly to the decline in consumption.

The difficulties experienced during these years must therefore be seen in the context of the problems facing the industry at large. What is surprising is that Locke's, a relatively small distillery, survived beyond the 1920s, while many larger concerns went out of production. One possible explanation is that the company's size made it easier to reduce overheads during recessions.

TABLE 12
Duty Charged in Ireland per Proof Gallon

1909	14s/9d
1919	50s/-
1920	72s/6d
1939	82s/6d
1946	95s/-
1947	137s/-
1952	176s/-

Source: anon., *The Story of Irish Whiskey* (Dublin 1961).

TABLE 13
Shareholders in John Locke and Co., 1921–50

	1921	1929	1943	1950
Locke, James Harvey	2013			
Locke, Mary Hester	769	769	769	
Hope-Johnstone, Mary Evelyn	384	384	384	1842
Eccles, Florence Emily	384	384	1	1459
Costello/Coffey	134	134		
Locke J.H./Joyce/Batten	133	133		
Coffey	50	50	50	50
Hibernian Bank		2013	2013	
Batten/Henderson/Coffey		133	133	133
Locke Mary Hester/Cooney		133	133	
Dudley/Murphy/De Vere			383	333
Coffey/Eccles		134		
Cooney/Coffey				133
Dudley				50

Source: Companies Registration Office, Dublin, D. 1610.

After James Harvey's death, the board of the distillery changed. Mary Locke ('Muds') became a director, but her role in the company's affairs were limited. She remained a registered director of the company until her death in 1943, but for a number of years prior to this she had been confined to a nursing home. After 1943 her daughters, Mary and Florence, began to play a more active role on the board of the distillery. The actual management of the distillery became the responsibility of two men: Thomas Joseph Coffey, the chief distiller, and the secretary, Joseph Cooney. Both men had worked their way up through the company. They were the only members on the board who were familiar with the day-to-day running of the distillery (both held a limited number of shares by the late 1920s).[4]

Chief distiller had always been a highly respected position in the company. In the years prior to and during John Edward's and James Harvey's management, it was held by Walter Furlong. During the 1890s he became one of the directors of the distillery. Furlong, who was very tall, was always known locally as 'the big man'. He was succeeded as chief distiller by Thomas Coffey, a miser of the highest order.

There are a number of stories about Coffey's meanness. One person remembered sitting beside him as a young boy on a bus bound for Kilbeggan. Coffey on this occasion was wearing a blue serge suit. When this person grew up he spotted him again fifteen years later at Mass wearing the same blue serge suit with leather bindings on the cuffs and elbows. Coffey also had a very smart lemon-coloured crombie which he wore for fifty years so that the sleeves were worn right through. He used to go to Whelan's shop (twenty-five yards from the distillery) to buy an apple every day, but when the price of apples went from 5d to 6d he never bought another one. For a short period Coffey used to eat his lunch in the hotel but never went on Fridays because he thought fish was bad value for money. Soon he gave up hotel lunches for financial reasons and had his sister Mary (who was his housekeeper at Brusna House) buy two chops for him instead. But this cost-saving exercise was thwarted by a rise in meat prices. Coffey then said that good meat was wasted on an old man like him and thereafter he lived on corn beef. When he died, he left his painfully accumulated fortune (a six-figure sum) to a distant relative in the United States who had never been to Ireland and whom he had never met. Coffey was one of the people in the distillery who made a lot of money from the illicit trade during the Second World War. He is reputed to have invested this in stocks and shares.

Although sales of Irish whiskey remained sluggish during the 1930s, Locke's managed to increase its market share. The company's sales improved a little during the second half of the decade; this can be inferred from a modest growth in the profits made by the company, during a period when national output was stagnant. After turning in a loss for a number of years, the company made a small profit in 1932. Although profits remained small they rose

TABLE 14
Net Profit or Loss Made by John Locke and Co., 1930–9

1930	– £497	1935	+ £199
1931	– £83	1936	+ £1429
1932	+ £850	1937	+ £4658
1933	+ £1010	1938	+ £6532
1934	+ £1326	1939	+ £6694

Source: National Library, Ms 20065(1), Darley, Orphen, Mc Gillycuddy to Locke June 1947.

during the second half of the decade from £1429 in 1936 to £6694 in 1939.

In 1933 the prohibition laws in the USA were finally repealed, thereby opening up new possibilities for sales in the American market. The company secretary, Joseph Cooney, travelled in both Britain and the USA during this period to promote Locke's whiskey. Britain remained the most important market for exports since Locke's had retained a number of customers there over the years; some of them first bought whiskey from the company in the last decades of the nineteenth century. During the 1930s new agencies were set up and more sophisticated advertising techniques were applied both in Ireland and in Britain in order to extend the company's trade. This was rewarded with a small degree of success. In March 1938 the secretary noted in correspondence that 'the company has been doing better of late'.[5] Another indication of the growing confidence of the board and management was the construction of a new warehouse to the west of Colgan's loft between 1937 and 1938.[6]

John Edward's eldest daughter, Mary Evelyn (Sweet), became a director of the company in 1939, at the age of fifty-seven. After her mother's death in 1943 she took the chair at the board meetings of the company. At this point it is worth sketching out some of the details of her earlier life. She had spent much of her adolescence hunting under the watchful eye of her mother and uncle Jim (James Harvey);

in time she became a highly accomplished rider, hunting side-saddle. There are a number of faded pictures of her in her early twenties in long black hunting skirts and riding boots. Despite the many moves she made around the British Isles in the course of her life, she was always a prominent member of the local hunt. It was within Meath hunting circles that she met a young army man from Mullingar, John Beardmore Batten, whom she married in London in 1910. Batten was in the Royal Fusiliers. His father, who was from Bristol, had also been in the British army, rising to the rank of colonel.

The marriage between Mary Evelyn and Batten provides another clue to the social circles within which the Lockes now moved. Fox-hunting was the social cement which brought together the landlords, gentry and the middle classes of Meath and Westmeath. Catholics, Protestants, Dissenters, Irish, English and Anglo-Irish found common ground on the field. While the sport was still a Protestant stronghold, Catholics with social status like the Lockes were accepted. Social life organized around the hunting calendar provided the basis for many marriages which crossed the religious divide. The hunting set was racy, colourful, even a little promiscuous by the standards of the time. The chase became the main social focus for Sweet and Flo, and they both wed army men of English extraction whom they met thereby.

Soon after Sweet's marriage she had a son named John who later had some involvement on the board of the company. This was not a success as John was a rolling stone by nature; he never spent much time in Ireland. When he was growing up the family lived at Lynn Lodge near Mullingar. Batten was called to arms in 1914. Because of his social status and the carnage of the trenches, he rose rapidly through the ranks, ultimately becoming a colonel. He was wounded and was lucky to survive, but the horror of war brought something of a change over him and in the aftermath his relationship to Sweet seems to have suffered.

Their marriage ended in the mid-1920s. Sweet was like her mother, lively, gregarious and outgoing, too much so perhaps for the colonel. She had no model of stable marriage because of the split between her own parents in her early childhood, and it was against her nature to suffer. It was said locally that she swopped husbands during a hunt in Westmeath. Her new husband, Mr Hope-Johnstone, whom she called Roguey, was eminently more suited to her. (*His* wife married Sir Thomas Ainsworth, whose spouse in turn became Lady Holmpatrick.) He was a dashing young Scot who was the master of the Westmeaths. Inevitably the Church strongly disapproved of this second marriage in October 1926, especially since Roguey was on his third round. As a result, shortly after her separation from the colonel, Sweet and her new husband moved to Lockerbie in Scotland, where they could continue the sporting life away from clerical scrutiny.

Sweet remained in Scotland until after her mother's death in 1943, despite the fact that she was already a director of the company at this stage. Upon her return she briefly lived in Mullingar before finally settling near Mallow in County Cork. The decision to live here was probably precipitated by the desire to remain away from Westmeath, where her relationship with Roguey was frowned upon. But the fact that hunting was good in Cork, Limerick and Tipperary probably also influenced their decision. The pair of them cut quite a dash across Munster. Her sister, Mrs Eccles, also became a director after their mother's death. Although she held a significant number of shares she seems to have played a relatively minor role on the distillery board. By nature she had a more reserved disposition than her elder sister.[7] During these years, consequently, the control of the business fell entirely into the hands of the management.

With the outbreak of the Second World War in 1939 the demand for whiskey rose. Because of the recession in the industry of previous decades most Irish distillers had laid down only limited stocks for maturation, and so there were limited stocks of mature Irish whiskey available for consumption. The other reason why stocks were scarce at Locke's was that they were being siphoned off to supply the illicit trade during the war years. The company was therefore not in a position to take advantage of the upswell in demand, and lost an opportunity to boost its financial standing.[8] Output and sales began to increase only towards the end of the war. In 1941 Locke's output was about 44,500 gallons, less than it had been in the 1908-9 season, but it climbed rapidly over the following years (see table 15).

The consumption of whiskey in Ireland rose between 1940 and 1950 from 479,824 proof gallons to 747,719 proof gallons. Exports (which were very significant during this period) rose from 253,208 proof gallons to 479,824 proof gallons. Locke's sales rose from £45,817 to £97,233

TABLE 15
Sales of Lockes and Duty Paid to the Revenue 1941-6

	PRODUCTION	SALES (INCLUDES DUTY)	DUTY
1941	44,551 p.g.*	£45,817	£24,841
1942	59,562 p.g.*	£105,176	£33,211
1943	78,831 p.g.*	£96,552	£43,955
1944	90,533 p.g.	£117,608	£50,480
1945	93,868 p.g.	£145,912	£67,666
1946	112,343 p.g.	£160,060	£82,628
1947	89,003 p.g.		
1948	120,978 p.g.		
1949	113,846 p.g.	£84,042	
1950	117,184 p.g.	£97,233	
1951	109,276 p.g.	£174,434	
1952		£85,622	

*calculated from duty paid in 1944.

Source: National Library, Ms 20065(1), Locke to Kean 8 September 1949; Darley, Orphen, Mc Gillycuddy to Locke, June 1947. Ms 20068, Locke to Provincial Bank, 17 October 1950; Ms 20068(4), Provincial Bank to Dudley 18 November 1953; Ms 20068(3), Locke to Provincial Bank July 1952.

between 1940 and 1950. The increase in sales during and after the war years was a welcome relief. Sales rose to £160,060 in 1946, but peaked in 1951, when they reached £174,434, declining dramatically thereafter.

The growth of production during the war years was constrained to some extent by the shortage of fuel and barley. A marked increase in production took place only after the war. It can be seen from the figures above (table 15) that duty was a heavy burden, accounting for over 45 per cent of the gross receipts from sales. The figures in table 15 show only the sales on which duty was paid. According to people who worked in the distillery, a large amount of Locke's whiskey was sold illicitly during the war years. The shortage of spirits on the market during these years drove up the price of whiskey, producing conditions which were particularly profitable for illicit distilling.

The principal shareholders of the company were unaware of the illicit trade, since they took little heed of the everyday running of the business. Old 'Muds' Locke was confined to a nursing home at this stage, where the management saw to it that she was looked after like royalty. Her daughters, Sweet and Flo, lived far from the distillery, leaving all responsibilities to the management. During the war years a number of people in the management of the distillery became involved in a fairly major illicit trade in whiskey. They had the full cooperation of an excise officer who was working at the distillery; without his involvement this type of fraud would have been impossible.

In the course of the war these people made small fortunes from defrauding the revenue. By operating a nightshift with the help of an excise officer, the illicit trade went undetected. Although a number of visiting excise officers were suspicious of the operation in Kilbeggan at this time, they were never there long enough to detect the fraud which was taking place on a massive scale. The volume of illicit spirits sold could be increased (unlike the legal trade) because much unmatured raw spirit was mixed with small amounts of mature spirit. This was bottled and then sold under the Locke's label as mature spirit.

During the night-shift, a lorry loaded with this contraband would leave the distillery to be sold in the west of Ireland, where it was least likely to be detected. Much of the workforce became implicated in this trade, most of them unwillingly. In an area where work was scarce employees had little choice but to keep the secret among themselves. Even today most of the surviving employees are reluctant to discuss the matter, and so this fraud passed unnoticed, despite the large number of people implicated in it. 'The Locke's Scandal' which followed attracted nation-wide attention, yet ironically related to a fraud which never actually happened.

THE LOCKE'S SCANDAL

After the Second World War there was a major shortage of mature whiskey on the British market, so the stocks at Locke's distillery became extremely valuable. In 1947 Mrs Hope-Johnstone and Mrs Eccles decided to take advantage of this and sell the distillery as a 'going concern'. In April and May of that year it was advertised in various trade journals and a number of offers were made over the next months (including one from Cooney, the company secretary), but were turned down as inadequate. Finally, a syndicate called the Trans-World Trust of Lausanne expressed an interest in the distillery. The main person behind this syndicate was a Swiss businessman, named Eindiguer, and an Englishman, Horace Henry Smith, who was his interpreter. Eindiguer had met Thomas Morris, a Clonmel solicitor, in Switzerland. Morris was extensively involved in greyhound coursing, and was helping Eindiguer to investigate the possibilities of bringing this sport to Switzerland. He had informed Eindiguer of the impending sale of the distillery.

The syndicate came to Ireland in September 1947, employing Stokes and Quirke (auctioneers) to negotiate the purchase. Quirke (who was then a prominent Fianna

Fáil senator) visited the distillery with Smith, Eindiguer and Morris. Eindiguer subsequently put in a tender of £305,000 for the distillery, which was accepted and a contract was drawn up and signed by both parties. The Department of Trade and Industry provided something of a sweetener to the buyers by granting an application for an increase of the distillery's export quota.

All seemed to be in order until the £75,000 deposit was not paid by the date agreed in the contract. By October Quirke and Morris became suspicious of the syndicate's financial standing. The police and officials from the Department of Justice were called in to investigate. Eindiguer was tracked down in a Dún Laoghaire hotel. His passport was checked and was found to be in order. On the following day he left Ireland, never to return. Later that day Smith was picked up by the police. They found a false passport in his possession; his real name was Alexander Maximoe. Maximoe was wanted by the British police for a number of criminal offences; he was therefore deported to England. But on the journey on the ferry to Holyhead he disappeared. It was assumed that he had jumped overboard and drowned. However, Maximoe had arranged for a boat to pick him up, so he successfully pulled off another close escape from the British police.

None of this attracted much attention from the general public until the young Laois-Offaly TD Oliver J. Flanagan accused some Fianna Fáil TDs, ministers and senators of being personally involved in a very shady plan to sell off Locke's distillery to 'foreigners'. This plot, according to Flanagan, involved bribery and corruption and was illegal. The allegation which attracted most attention concerned two gold watches (presumably Swiss made), which Quirke advised Eindiguer to present to the Taoiseach, de Valera, and his son, as a token of his esteem. Soon, half the country was talking about Dev's gold watch, and the various other allegations and smears which were being slung around the Dáil. The reputation of Fianna Fáil was at an all-time low at this stage. As the Locke's scandal unfolded, it was seen by the general public as simply one more example of how individuals within the party were using political power to feather their own nests. In response, Éamon de Valera appointed a Tribunal on 7 November 1947 to investigate these allegations. The Tribunal began to take on a much higher public profile than Fianna Fáil anticipated, and it became clear that if these allegations were proved to be true, the political costs for the government could be extremely high.[9]

Forty-nine people gave evidence to the Tribunal. It became apparent that 60,000 gallons of whiskey from the distillery were going to be sold on the English black market for £11 a gallon,[10] the syndicate earning a sum of about £660,000 (after purchasing the distillery for £305,000). But the most serious allegations were those which accused ministers in the government of facilitating this deal and of having a personal interest in it. While it seems apparent that the additional export quota was granted in an improper manner, the Tribunal decided that no minister had any knowledge of the dubious intentions of the syndicate. It concluded therefore on 18 December that the allegations were entirely without foundation.[11]

The Tribunal was particularly scathing in regard to the integrity of Flanagan. The High Court judges found it

quite impossible to follow or appreciate the Deputy Flanagan's evershifting evidence as to the meaning to be attached to the allegation that a minister of state had a keen personal interest in the sale of the distillery. There is not a scintilla of evidence that any minister had a particle of such interest. The charge is an extremely grave one. We are satisfied that it is wholly untrue, that it is entirely without foundation and it was made with a degree of recklessness amounting to complete irresponsibility ...

We found it necessary to exercise extreme caution in dealing with the evidence of Deputy Flanagan. We found him very uncandid and much disposed to answer questions unthinkingly and as if he were directing his replies elsewhere than to the Tribunal. On several occasions he contradicted himself and was disposed to shift his ground, when he found that answers already given would lead him where he did not wish to go. He was on other occasions in conflict with testimony which we believe to be true. In respect of two matters we are satisfied that he told us what he knew to be untrue.

The deputies who had vociferously supported Flanagan's claims in the Dáil were conspicuously absent from the Tribunal. Therefore, Flanagan's only witnesses were the company secretary, Joseph Cooney, and his son. Unfortunately for him, there were major contradictions between his evidence and theirs.[12]

Initially the publication of the report seemed to take the pressure off de Valera's Fianna Fáil government. But when an election was called for the 4 February 1948 the results proved otherwise: Fianna Fáil lost eight seats. To rub salt into the wound, Oliver J. Flanagan topped the poll in Laois-Offaly with 14,370 votes; he attracted even more votes than Lemass and de Valera who had consistently been the country's poll-toppers in Dublin and Clare respectively. Fine Gael won an extra seat and the new party, Clann na Poblachta, won ten. The result led to the first inter-party government. While the Locke's Scandal was not the only factor in the government's downfall, it swung the balance towards the opposition parties by galvanizing anti-Fianna Fáil sentiment. The transferable vote amplified the impact of the swing against Fianna Fáil.[13] The notoriety which the distillery attracted in the wake of the scandal is well captured in a ballad which appeared shortly afterwards in the *Carrick Opinion* at the time of the wedding of Princess Elizabeth (now Queen Elizabeth):

> We have got so pally lately with our friends across the sea,
> That I thought the Royal Couple would ask an odd TD
> To be present at their wedding just to show they bear no malice,
> And last night I had an awful dream, the Dáil was in the Palace.
>
> I could see Dev in all his glory, in a tie of Orange and Green,
> While he wore a great big Shamrock in his brilliant white Caubeen,
> He was arm in arm with Dillon and Sir Basil Brooke was near,
> And all three of them were toasting Sean McBride in English Beer.
> I could hear Lemass and Aiken calling Attlee 'Dear old Clem',
> While a Fianna Fáil Back-Bencher said the Princess was a Gem,

And all was going gaily 'till an MP from the Docks,
Shouted 'Pass the Whiskey Oliver – make sure you give me Locke's'.

It was then the ructions started and I heard a piercing scream,
As I jumped to dodge a flower-pot and woke up from my Dream.[14]

Whatever the broader political implications of the scandal, it may have made it impossible for Locke's to secure a partner who could have brought an injection of badly needed capital into the business. This forced the company to depend on its own meagre resources during the following years when a major effort was made to restore the fortunes of the business.

NOTES

1. R. Weir, 'In and out of Ireland, The Distillers Company Ltd ... 1900–39', *Irish Economic and Social History,* vol. vii, pp. 45–8; R. Weir, 'Rationalization and Diversification in the Scotch Whisky Industry, 1900–1939', *Economic History Review*, vol. xlii, no. 3, pp. 378–93.
2. National Library, Ms 20072(6), Memorandum for Meeting with the Transport and General Workers Union; Ms 20072(3). Details of John Locke and Co. (typescript); Companies Registration Office, Dublin, 1610/16.
3. J. Nettleton, *The Manufacture of Spirits in the UK* (London 1893); Michael Byrne, 'The Distilling Industry in Co. Offaly, 1780–1954', in H. Murtagh, *Irish Midland Studies* (Athlone 1980), p. 226.
4. Companies Registration Office, 1610/31, 1610/34, 1610/42.
5. National Library, Ms 20079, Secretary to Miley and Miley. Locke's Tribunal, Cooney's evidence.
6. Indenture, 1 December 1937, Barry and Butler to Locke (in possession of Bernard Mc Evoy, for Cooley Distillery).
7. Mullingar Library, typed manuscript relating to the Locke family; National Library, Ms 20073, Hibernian Bank to Locke, 14 August 1939; Companies Registration Office, D. 1610/12, D. 1610/36, D. 1610/42.
8. National Library, Ms 20072(6), Memorandum *op cit*, Ms 20072(3), Details of John Locke and Co.
9. National Library, Ms 949–52, Locke Tribunal, vol. 1. p. 1. J. Lee, *Ireland 1912–1985, Politics and Society* (Cambridge 1989), pp. 296–7; B. Ó hEithir, *The Begrudger's Guide to Irish Politics* (Dublin 1986), pp. 115–18,

10. Locke's was insured for fire in 1946 with a policy that covered them for £178,130. £42,690 of this was for their buildings, £20,740 was for equipment and the rest was for their stocks of whiskey. National Library, Ms 20078(1–2), Insurance policies, 1917–54.
11. National Library, Locke's Tribunal, *op cit.*
12. Lee, pp. 296–7, Ó hEithir.
13. *Ibid.*
14. I would like to thank Raymond Anthony for sending in this ballad from the *Carrick Opinion*. Raymond remembered collecting jars of Locke's whiskey from the railway station in Fiddown for his parents' pub at Owning, Piltown, Co. Kilkenny.

7

'SLIPPING ALL ALONG THE LINE'
1949–1958

When the dust finally settled on 'the Locke's Scandal' the owners abandoned all ideas of selling the distillery. They decided to overhaul the whole business, which was in a shambles at this stage. Repairs and replacements had constantly been deferred because of the poor financial standing of the distillery. With the exception of the construction of a new warehouse in the 1930s, hardly any money had been invested in the company since it was incorporated in 1893. But despite all these problems Locke's still retained a niche in the market, especially among connoisseurs of fine whiskey. One such connoisseur was Winston Churchill, who had a particular liking for the taste of Locke's. The old war-horse is reputed to have said that it was as 'mellow and pure as nature's breath'.[1]

Another discerning drinker who had a taste for Locke's whiskey was Brian O'Nolan (alias Myles na cGopaleen or Flann O'Brien), whose in-depth knowledge of whiskey was largely due to the fact that his father was an excise officer. This job brought the family to Tullamore in 1920 when Brian was only nine years old. His father supervised the collection of excise duties from D.E. Williams in Tullamore and Locke's in Kilbeggan. Anthony Cronin, O'Nolan's biographer, argues that the countryside around Tullamore and Kilbeggan provided the setting for his novel *The Third Policeman*. He subsequently referred to Locke's in his *Irish Times* column 'Cruiskeen Lawn' on a number of occasions. He often used to annoy publicans with his knowledge of the law governing the proof strength of whiskey. Disputes broke out with barmen when he suspected that water had been mixed into the bottle from which his ball of malt had been taken. He would sometimes produce a hydrometer from his inside pocket and immerse it in his glass with all the clientele looking on. But this habit caused such consternation and conflict that he gave it up.[2]

There is an interesting reference to Locke's in *The Hard Life*. The hero, Mr Collopy, talked at length about life and death and the universe from his kitchen armchair after indulging in his favourite whiskey:

Mr Collopy was slumped in his cane armchair, the steel-rimmed glasses far down his nose. In an easy chair opposite was Father Kurt Fahrt who was a very tall man, thin, ascetic, grey-haired, blue about the jaws, with a neck so slender that there would be room, so to speak, for two of them inside his priestly collar. On the edge of the range, handy to the reach, of those philosophers, was a glass. On the floor beside Mr Collopy's chair was what was known as 'the crock'. It was in fact a squat earthenware container, having an ear on each side, in which the Kilbeggan Distillery marketed its wares. The Irish word for whiskey – Uisge Beatha – were burnt into its face. This vessel was, of course, opaque and therefore mysterious; one could not tell how empty or full it was, nor how much Mr Collopy had been drinking.[3]

The same crock surfaced later in the novel in another informative conversation between Collopy and Father Fahrt, when the crock was almost empty:

– The man whose aim is to smooth out the path of the human race cannot easily fail.
– Well, I hope that's true. Give me your glass.
Here new drinks were decanted with sacramental piety and precision.
– It's a queer thing, Father Fahrt mused, that men in my position have again and again to attack the same problem, solve it, and yet find that the solution is never any easier to reach. Next week I have to give a retreat at Kinnegad. After that, other retreats at Kilbeggan and Tullamore.
– Hah! Kilbeggan? That's where my little crock here came from, refilled a hundred times since. And emptied a hundred times too, by gob.[4]

The rather run-down, shambolic state of Locke's at this time, and the embarrassment the scandal caused for the Fianna Fáil government, seems to have had a certain appeal to Flann O'Brien, quite apart from the fact that he was one of the distillery's most indulgent customers.

Apart from being severely under-capitalized, it is quite evident from the business records that the company also suffered from bad management. In 1948-9, for example, the distilling season had to be extended because of the poor condition of the plant; one of the wash backs was leaking badly and had to replaced, the worm tubs were leaking, one of the main valves failed, and there was a shortage of casks. With the extension of the season the old steam engine had to be brought into use since the river was dry (the waterwheel still provided ninety per cent of power required). Using the steam engine over a prolonged period was costly as coal prices had risen dramatically.[5] Distilling out of season created a number of other problems; it reduced the income from the sale of spent grains for example, since grass provided farmers with all their feeding requirements for animals during the summer months.

Problems on the production side of the business were compounded by poor sales on the Irish market. There were also problems getting export licences, which prevented Locke's from extending their sales in Britain. Poor government policy in this sphere was damaging potential sales in Britain, where Locke's enjoyed a buoyant demand for mature whiskey. The company was able to show a profit at this stage largely because of its British sales.[6]

As noted in chapter five, the rule-of-thumb methods used in the production of whiskey at Locke's had continued relatively unchanged since the nineteenth century. Nobody, including the chief distiller, had any formal training in the fundamental principles of distilling which had changed production methods considerably elsewhere. It was with this problem in mind that the board appointed J.J. Hogan to the position of assistant distiller. Hogan had a thorough training in the latest alcohol production techniques with Ceimicí Teo, the highly modern state-run alcohol company which had distilleries at Cooley, Labbadish,

Carrickmacross and Carndonagh. Hogan, who arrived in March 1949, played a major role in improving production at Kilbeggan over the following years.[7] This was the first occasion that Locke's had a connection with Ceimicí Teo. (Some fifty years later Cooley Distillery, the new Irish whiskey company, began distilling in the former Ceimicí Teo plant at Cooley. This whiskey is matured in Locke's distillery.)

In 1949 a new secretary, H.M. Greene, was also appointed. The duties of general manager and secretary were divided at this point and Joseph Cooney took up the position of general manager. The book-keeping system was overhauled and updated and J. Marshall Dudley was co-opted onto the board. He participated more than previous board members in running the distillery.[8]

Over the next few years about £55,000 was invested in modernizing the plant; this improved the productive capacity of the distillery. The grain-handling facilities were overhauled and concurrent brewing and distilling was introduced. To increase warehouse space, the T-Siphon building was erected in 1949 using direct labour; the unusual design, based on a building in the ancient city of Ure in Iraq, being provided by a graduate of Trinity College Dublin on his first assignment.. All of these improvements to the buildings and plant were financed predominantly by extending the company's bank overdraft. By December 1950 it had risen to £33,293. In order to partly cover this, £19,000 of the company's debentures had already been reissued to the Provincial Bank in College St, Dublin, in the mid-1940s.[9] Although improvements on the production side were made, there was little development in the area of advertising and marketing. In the year ending June 1953, for example, the company spent only £1484 in this area; more than this had been spent on advertising prior to the First World War.[10]

The improvements to the plant helped matters somewhat. New Wilton Furnaces meant that cheap low-grade peat drawn from the local bogs could be used under the stills instead of expensive high-grade coal,[11] which sent huge clouds of black smoke over the town almost visible in Mullingar. This was highly inefficient as most of the heat went up the chimney. Many of the older people still remember a black fog hanging over the town when certain weather conditions prevailed. Apart from reducing over-heads, the turf also provided a more even heat to the stills, which improved the whiskey. In addition, the still bottoms were not burnt out so quickly, and the brickwork did not need to be regularly repaired. The use of coal meant that new firebars had to be cast regularly by a local moulder named Rooney, who had a forge near the town.[12]

The company continued to employ a number of crafts-men for maintenance and repair work. They employed a back builder (Mike Smith), and a carpenter (Jack Moore). A fitter who carried out electrical work, plumbing, copper-work and soldering was also taken on in 1949. He had pre-viously worked with Hogan in Ceimicí Teo. More tradi-tional skills were retained in the distillery forge where a blacksmith (Farrell) was always on call. The coopers repaired the casks sent by customers, but they did not make new ones. Two millers, who dressed the millstones, were also employed. One of them, Barney Finn, was the only person left in the distillery who knew how to start up the old steam engine.[13]

A number of Irish companies did installation and repair work at Locke's; Tonge and Taggart of Dublin, for exam-ple, cast new plates for the mash tuns; Millar's of Dublin continued to repair the stills, and the GNR Railway Works in Dundalk did some brasswork. Craig's Engineering Works of Derry put in new elevators and steeping tanks. But most of the actual machinery and the specialist advice on plant came from Britain.[14]

Despite these improvements the business was still strug-gling in 1952. Sales continued to be disappointing and the cost of raw materials was rising. As if these problems weren't enough, the budget in April 1952 came down very heavily on the distilling industry. Duty on whiskey increased from 137 shillings a proof gallon to 176 shillings. This led to a considerable fall in consumption.[15] After the budget, publicans tended to concentrate on the more heavily advertised brands like Jameson's and Power's, cutting back on the smaller brands like Locke's. The consequent decline in sales meant that the distillery was no longer able to meet the cost of its overheads. Stocks began to build up in the warehouses. It was decided that only a small season of whiskey would be made in 1952–3. The distillery no longer made a profit after the 1952 budget, and by November 1953 its bank overdraft had risen to £44,000. It became increasingly difficult to secure capital to pay the duty on sales leaving the warehouses. This problem became particularly acute prior to Christmas 1953, a time which seasonally brought an increase in orders.[16]

Morale was low at this stage. Greene, the company secretary, resigned in November 1953, as he was angered by the attitude of Mrs Hope-Johnstone towards company matters. On the same day Hogan was informed that the company was compelled to dispense with his services as a distiller. Distilling, therefore, ceased in Kilbeggan in 1953. However, Hogan remained at Locke's for a few more years doing various jobs including administration, before moving on to take up the post of distiller with Power's in Dublin. Coffey had resigned as a director in May of that year, and Major John Batten (son of Mrs Hope-Johnstone) was appointed to replace him. Another family member, Dennis Eccles (the son of Flo), had married into the Murphy family (Independent Newspapers etc.) and from about 1940 onwards there was always a Murphy represented on the board. Another family member, Cyril McCormack (the son of Count John McCormack, the singer), who had married Patricia (the daughter of Flo), also began to work for the distillery, promoting Locke's whiskey in the USA. He became a director in 1955. But it was difficult to sell pot still whiskey in the

States, as Americans had a preference for lighter Scotch blends which were predominantly made up from patent still whiskey. Attempts were therefore made to secure either a patent still or at least a supply of grain spirit from Gilbeys or Ceimicí Teo. Neither of these plans came to anything.[17]

It is difficult to know if the acquisition of a patent still would have been the panacea to all the company's problems. Tullamore acquired a patent still at the end of the 1940s, but it closed in 1954. Economic circumstances in Ireland were not good during these years; this combined with the heavy duty on whiskey made it difficult for Locke's to maintain their sales on the Irish market. The secretary wrote to Mrs Hope-Johnstone in September 1954: 'we appear to be slipping all along the line ... sales of Irish whiskey have slumped to such an extraordinary level'.[18]

Little progress was being made in marketing Locke's in the USA. Sales on the British market, which had shown some promise, had fallen dramatically from £19,197 in 1950–1 to only £7150 in 1952–3. The fall in UK demand was partly a consequence of a rise in duty in 1952 and partly because Scotch came off the ration system in that year. The distillers in the Irish Republic failed to co-operate with each other on the export market. In the absence of a combined Irish effort in this sphere, the Scotch distillers (who did co-operate) were now able to undermine completely the Irish export trade. Locke's suffered from this general malaise within the Irish industry. The export trade to Britain had been important to Locke's, representing almost 20 per cent of the value of its sales in 1950–1. In the 1952–3 season, British exports fell to just over 8 per cent of the company's sales. By September 1955 Mrs Hope-Johnstone was informed by the management that 'our prospects of regaining lost ground ... are now rather remote, particularly as there appears to be a grave shortage of money'.[19]

The Provincial Bank remained reasonably sympathetic to

the company's predicament. But when the manager died in 1956, his successor was less accommodating. The company's overdraft had risen to £52,000 by the end of 1956. Its total liabilities (including £12,000 owed to the Revenue Commissioners) amounted to £67,000. By 1957 the bank refused to make any further advances, taking the view that since Gilbey's were unlikely to invest any capital in the distillery it was unlikely that it could be restored to profitability. In March 1957 the board of the bank wished to know exactly 'what the company now has in mind regarding the business and its commitments to the bank'.[20]

A last-ditch attempt was made to save the distillery in 1958. Cyril Count McCormack, who was at this stage the US representative for the Irish Industrial Development Authority, tried to entice American businessmen to invest in Locke's, but they seemed no more inclined to get involved than their Irish or British counterparts.[21]

The fate of the distillery was finally sealed on 27 November 1958. Five years earlier the company had issued a registered debenture in favour of the bank in order to secure and extend its overdraft. The money secured by this debenture became payable on 26 November 1958. The following day the bank called in the receiver under the powers contained in the debenture of 1953.[22]

The closure of Locke's distillery seems to have been a consequence of the declining demand for pot still whiskey. In this context, perhaps the real question is why the distillery survived as long as it did? When the Irish potable market collapsed in the 1920s, the future looked bleak for small distillers like Locke's. British social attitudes towards alcohol had changed over the previous decades. Anti-drink campaigns and high taxation reduced consumption considerably. Alcoholic drinks fell from second to fifth place in the league of consumer expenditure between 1900 and 1939. Even the Scotch industry suffered serious setbacks between 1900 and the mid-1930s, and the introduction of Prohibition in America prevented any possibility of opening up new markets to compensate for the loss of sales at home.[23] In the face of these developments a large part of the Irish distilling industry went out of business, including all of the major patent still producers in Ulster. But by the 1930s, Locke's was one of the five remaining distilleries in the Free State. In the circumstances, this was a significant achievement. Having weathered the storm, however, the management seemed unable to place the distillery on a sound financial footing.

There was a market for Locke's whiskey both in Ireland and in Britain. But the company needed better advertising and marketing techniques. While some argue that any publicity is better than no publicity, the scandal does not seem to have contributed to the goodwill of the business. The company desperately needed a partner to increase investment in the distillery plant, which was run down, and in advertising and marketing. The ownership and management failed to seek such a partnership. When they eventually began to do so in the 1950s, it was too late, as the distillery's reputation was tarnished. The illicit trade carried out by various members of the management during the war years also contributed to the financial difficulties of the business. Valuable stocks were depleted by this trade so the distillery was unable to take full advantage of the upturn in the market during and after the war. Good trade during this period may have assisted the company to sort out its financial problems and thereby have enabled it to cope with the down-turn after the 1952 budget. In this respect, the greed of a few who made fortunes from the illicit trade caused immense damage to the business. Bad (and untrustworthy) management in the 1940s prevented the company from achieving high sales when market demand had rose.

The government's industrial policy was extremely poor in regard to the distilling industry. The government failed to give the sufficient export quotas to Irish distillers during periods when it had the possibility of extending sales in Britain, thinking that exports would diminish revenue yield from the home trade. The increase in the duty on spirits in the budget of 1952 was the final nail in the coffin of a distillery which depended primarily on sales within a depressed economy. These problems were compounded by poor management, the business was therefore no longer viable.

NOTES

1. Advertising material in the possession of Brian Quinn, Kilbeggan.
2. A. Cronin, *No laughing Matter: The Life and Times of Flann O'Brien* (London 1990), pp. 18, 207.
3. Flann O'Brien, *The Hard Life* (London 1990), p. 31.
4. *Ibid.*, pp. 52–3.
5. National Library, Ms 20087, Secretary's Report, June 1949.
6. National Library, Ms 20066(1), Secretary to Dudley, 17 January 1949; Ms 20085, Locke to CSO, 12 January 1950.
7. National Archives, Dublin, Irish Distillers Collection, P. 270, File on Hogan.
8. National Library, Ms 20066(2), Secretary to Dudley, 16 August 1949; Ms 20066(3), AGM Minutes, June 1949; Secretary's Report 1949, *op cit.*
9. National Library, Locke Tribunal, Balance Sheet, 30 June 1946; Ms 20068(1), Manager of Provincial Bank, College Green, Dublin, to Locke's, 12 December 1950; Ms 20072(2), Locke to Owtram, 5 November 1953.
10. In 1911, £1982 was spent on advertising; National Library, Ms 20029, General Expenses Book 1909–16; Ms 20068(4), Locke to Manager, Provincial Bank, 30 June 1953.
11. National Library, Ms 20120, Ms 20119, Ms 20002(1), correspondence about machinery.
12. Interview with J.J. Hogan.
13. *Ibid.*
14. National Library, Ms 20100(10), Locke's to Tonge and Taggart, 4 May 1951; Ms 20100(4), Locke's to Millar's, 10 February 1950; Ms 20087, Secretary's Report, June 1949; Ms 20100(10), 7 February 1952, Locke's to Mc Cormack; Tribunal, vol. 4, Valuation, February 1947; National Archives, Dublin, Irish Distillers Collection, P. 270, Craig to Locke's, 1, 21 March 1951. See other correspondence on machinery.
15. National Library, Ms 20065(2), Daly to Locke's, 30 May 1953; Ms 20068(3). See correspondence with manager of the Provincial Bank, Jan–June 1953.
16. National Library, Ms 20065(2), Locke's to Minister for Finance, 24

March 1953; Ms 20072(2), Locke to Beddy, 13 November 1953, and Locke to Owtram, 5 November 1953.

17. National Library, Ms 20066(10), Secretary to Hope-Johnstone, 17 November 1953; Ms 20068(3), Locke to manager, Provincial Bank, 4 May 1953; Ms 20066(14), Secretary to Hope-Johnstone, 29 September 1955; Ms 20066(19), Marshall Dudley to Locke's, 15 February 1956; National Archives, Irish Distillers Collection, P. 270, file relating to Hogan.

18. National Library, Ms 20066(12), Secretary to Mrs Hope-Johnstone, 6 September 1954.

19. National Library, Ms 20066(14), Locke's to Hope-Johnstone, 13 September 1955; Ms 20072(3), Locke to Scott, 18 January 1954; Byrne, *op cit*, p. 237.

20. National Library, Ms 20068(6), Provincial Bank to Cyril Count Mc Cormack, 1 March 1957; Ms 20072(5), 31 December 1956, Provincial Bank to Locke's.

21. National Library, Ms 20068(7), McCormack to Manager, Provincial Bank, 8 January, 26 February 1958.

22. Statutory Declaration on behalf of the Provincial Bank College St, document held by Dockrell Farrell, Solicitors, for Cooley Distillery; Companies Registration Office, 1610/44, 13 May 1953, 1610/57, 27 November 1958.

23. R. Weir, 'Rationalization and diversification in the Scotch whisky industry, 1900–1939', *Economic History Review*, vol. xlii, no. 3, 1989, pp. 378–9.

8

DORMANCY AND REVIVAL
1959–1992

In the years after 1958 the receiver sold off part of the stocks of mature whiskey and various other assets belonging to the business. He then sold the entire premises and whatever remained of the stocks in 1963 to Karl Heinz Mellor, for the sum of £10,000.[1] Mellor made a large profit by selling off the remainder of the stocks. Some was sold in Ireland, but most was sold in Germany by mail order under his own label, Old Galleon, at a considerable profit. The distillery was turned into a pigsty. Most of the crocks, which Flann O'Brien referred to in *The Hard Life*, were smashed up and used as a base in one of the new concrete floors which Mellor laid.

When the new owner moved to Kilbeggan the atmosphere at the distillery changed considerably. The old warehouses which had been used for generations for maturing whiskey were converted for pig-rearing. Fortunately most of the plant was left intact. Mellor also handed over what remained of the distillery's business records to the National Library. A truck was sent down from Dublin and the various ledgers, warehouse and corn books were loaded up and taken to Kildare Street, where they now reside in safe hands. The strong smell of maturing whiskey, and the smells of malting barley, the mash and fermentation which had for long been associated with the distillery were displaced by smells of a more odorous and pungent nature.

Mellor remained in possession of the distillery until 1969, when it was sold to a company called Powerscreen, which had the agency for Volvo loading shovels. Powerscreen required only part of the premises so most of the distillery lay idle over the next decade or so. But a small engineering works was set up in warehouse no. 1, where parts were made for Powerscreen.

Unfortunately some of the distilling plant was removed for its scrap value in the early 1970s. The four copper pot stills, the copper worms, the copper cooling system which lay in the bed of the millrace above the waterwheel, and various other items, were sold for £15,000. A week later the bottom dropped out of the copper market and the scrap dealer lost out on the deal. If copper prices had fallen a month earlier the equipment might have been saved. Most of the plant in the still house, the heart of the distillery, had been removed by the mid-1970s, including the charge tank. All that remained was the stone and brickwork. Fortunately, however, the licence to distil was maintained. Each year the owners paid £5 to the State to preserve the licence.

Token Grass Tongs rented the T-Siphon building and warehouse no. 3 from Powerscreen in the early 1980s for storing grain. The other buildings remained empty and the slow onset of decay began to take its toll on many of them. Powerscreen had an agency in Kilbeggan until 1988, when the company was sold to an English buyer. All the distillery property on the south-side of the road was sold to Brian Quinn (who had moved to Kilbeggan to work for Powerscreen). A large maltings beside Brusna House was knocked down at this stage since the structure had become dangerous.

In 1982 the Kilbeggan community began to take an interest in the distillery. Later that year the Kilbeggan Development Association received a caretaker's lease from Powerscreen and in the following year the major task of renovation began. Many people in the community made a contribution to this work, which was entirely voluntary in the first years. Money was raised by selling life membership of the museum for £200; in addition a number of fund-raising functions and raffles were held. The steam engine and mill buildings were the first priorities for renovation; in order to halt further decay this area was reroofed. The waterwheel was also renovated; three local timber mills provided the timber for the wheel. The renovation of the waterwheel was finished by May 1983 and during that month it turned for the first time in many years. This was perhaps the first landmark in the slow recovery of the distillery's fortunes.

In 1985 FÁS became involved, providing labour and some money for materials. A major restoration project got under way to renovate the fine old steam engine (built by Turnbull, Grant and Jack in Glasgow in 1887). The engine had been exposed to the elements for a number of years. Two ESB fitters began working on the restoration of the engine on a voluntary basis in 1985. It was taken apart and each piece was taken to a workshop off the premises where the rust was carefully removed. This process continued until each piece of the whole engine had been removed, cleaned, and returned; in the autumn of 1986 it was reassembled. A boiler was acquired in August of the following year and the engine was in working order again. After three years of painstaking work the steam engine finally came back to life; it had been idle for thirty-five years.[2]

By the end of 1987 the future prospects of the distillery had improved dramatically. Cooley Distillery Plc (which had been set up in 1987 to distil whiskey) became interested in Locke's because they needed bonded warehouses. John Locke and Co. was the last operative distillery in the Republic of Ireland which did not become part of Irish Distillers. Cooley Distillery Plc's involvement in Kilbeggan initiated a whole new phase of development which has revitalized the town's traditional connection with the distilling industry. This has led to a large investment in the buildings in Kilbeggan; a number of the fine old warehouses which had become very dilapidated were renovated and brought back into use, as was the cooperage. While Cooley have taken over a large part of the distillery, the Kilbeggan Community Association has obtained a lease on part of the old plant which is being preserved as a museum of industrial archaeology.

To understand current developments at Locke's it is necessary to look at the evolution of the Irish distilling industry in recent years and the decision by a group of entrepreneurs to open the first independent whiskey distillery in the twentieth century.

THE RECENT HISTORY OF
THE IRISH DISTILLING INDUSTRY

Since the closure of the large patent still distilleries in Belfast and Derry during the 1920s the Irish industry has never been able to develop an export market of any significance. The industry in Ireland by the 1960s was entirely based on pot still production; there were no column stills in operation. The surviving distilling dynasties in Ireland, Jameson's, Power's, and Cork Distillers, were loath to move away from traditional pot still production, and so it had never been possible to increase sales of Irish whiskey on the American market, as Americans had always preferred lighter grain whiskey like those made by the Scotch industry. As one exasperated whiskey marketing executive once said, 'Americans knew that they did not like Irish whiskey, but they had never tasted it.'

Because the Irish distilling industry was restricted to pot still production, it was impossible to achieve economies of scale. In order to overcome this problem and to increase competitiveness, the three surviving distilling companies in the Republic of Ireland decided to amalgamate in 1966 into one company, Irish Distillers. In the early 1970s they bought the only distillery in the North, Bushmills, thereby creating a monopoly. Irish Distillers then embarked on a large investment programme to reduce production costs. The Power and Jameson distilleries in Dublin were closed down and all operations were moved to Midleton in Co.

Cork, where a large new distillery was built. The closure of these remaining distilleries in Dublin brought to a close a long and glorious distilling tradition. The old Cork Distillers Company distillery in Midleton was also closed down. The new plant included both patent and pot stills and since then most of the brands made by Irish Distillers have largely been made up of grain whiskey blended with a small amount of pot still whiskey. Irish Distillers had therefore overcome one of the major barriers to the growth of the Irish industry. They could now achieve economies of scale by using the patent stills in their new plant, and also by managing one large company as opposed to three small ones.

Having overcome the major production problems, Irish Distillers now faced another barrier, marketing. International brand marketing is difficult and Irish Distillers found it hard to compete. Not one of its brands has a place in the top 100 spirit brands in the world. Irish Distillers found it difficult to gain access to international distribution networks. Over the years international spirits marketing became more concentrated as five companies, Allied Lyons (UK), Grand Metropolitan (UK), Guinness (UK), Suntory (Japan), and Seagram's (Canada), came to dominate the world branded spirits industry. To put this in perspective, the US is the largest export market for Irish whiskey, yet it accounts for less than 10 per cent of their sales. Irish whiskey exports are less than 1 per cent of Scotch exports.

In 1987 a consortium of the three UK-based multinational drinks companies made a take-over bid for Irish Distillers. The bid was fought by the company. Pernod-Ricard, a French drinks company, entered the take-over battle. After a spectacular series of moves, including pleadings before the Supreme Court, Pernod-Ricard won total control. Ownership of Irish Distillers passed into French hands.

Pernod brought important international marketing and distribution skills to the sale of Irish whiskey. Between 1987 and 1992, exports grew, particularly in the emerging markets of Southern Europe and the Far East.

COOLEY DISTILLERY ENTERS THE FRAY

The idea to set up a new distillery in Ireland to compete with Irish Distillers was largely the brain-child of John Teeling. Doctor Teeling's interest in distilling goes back to 1970 when he carried out a study at Harvard on marketing Irish whiskey. In 1986 he looked into the possibility of buying out Irish Distillers. Although nothing came of this plan, Teeling saw that there was plenty of room for expansion within the Irish distilling industry. The Irish Distillers Group had a poor marketing record because of their lack of distribution strength; they still sell about half of their output in Ireland. Ireland accounts for only about 0.1 per cent of the world market for whiskey, so the company's only hope of expanding is to compete on international markets.

In 1987 Cooley purchased for £120,000 the state-owned Ceimicí Teo distillery at Cooley in Co. Louth, which had closed in 1986. A further £3,000,000 was spent installing pot and patent stills. This acquisition enabled the company to set up a high-tech production facility. In addition, the company came to an agreement with the owners of Locke's distillery in Kilbeggan whereby Cooley acquired the assets in return for shares in Cooley Distillery Plc.

Along with the distilleries at Cooley and Kilbeggan, the company acquired equipment from the Tullamore distillery which closed in 1954. Significantly, it included the pot stills, which were moved to Kilbeggan. During the next phase of development the company hopes to recommence pot still production at Locke's. Cooley have also acquired the use of one of D.E. Williams' warehouses in Tullamore.

Cooley also acquired the brand names of John Locke and Co. of Kilbeggan and Andrew A. Watt and Co. of Derry (established 1762 and closed 1937). The principal shareholders at this stage, apart from John Teeling, were Lee Mallaghan, Donal Kinsella and John Power. Essentially Teeling put together both the logical concept of the whole project and the early finance. Mallaghan's entry enabled

Cooley to make use of Locke's distillery in Kilbeggan, while Power and Kinsella provided much of the initial financial backing. All four partners had previously been associated through their involvement in the mining industry. The distilling assets acquired by this group were all transferred into Cooley Distillery Plc, which was duly incorporated in 1987, and two years later whiskey production began. By 1990 Cooley was producing 250,000 cases of pure pot still malt whiskey and 650,000 cases of patent still grain whiskey per annum.

According to Irish law, the new spirit produced in a whiskey distillery needs to mature for at least three years before it can be called whiskey. This requires extensive storage and finance. Cooley's demand for warehousing is constantly increasing. The warehouses at Locke's play a key role in the maturation of the spirits made by the company. When the distillation process is complete, the new spirit is taken by tanker from the distillery in Co. Louth to Kilbeggan in Co. Westmeath. Cooley has most of its filling and coopering facilities at Locke's, and also a number of warehouses.

At the cooperage in Kilbeggan, coopers recruited from Scotland prepare oak casks for filling, which have already been used once in the USA. US regulations dictate that bourbon casks can be used only once in the USA and have to be made from new oak wood. This situation has been exploited by Irish and Scotch distillers, who purchase most of the casks after they have been used once. Irish and Scottish regulations stipulate that the casks must be made of oak; their age, or the number of times they have been used, is immaterial. In the Kilbeggan cooperage these American casks are overhauled and charred (which gives the whiskey its colour). Then they are filled and sealed and dispatched to whichever warehouse they are to be bonded in.

All the warehouses which have been brought back into use at Locke's are now full. They contain over 15,000 40-gallon casks. These slightly damp old stone warehouses are the ideal environment for maturing whiskey in the traditional fashion; conditions during the maturation phase have a significant influence on the taste. Very little Irish whiskey is now matured in warehouses like this. Locke's distillery holds more stocks now than at any time during its history.

The distilling industry has been one of the great lost opportunities of the Irish industrial sector. For centuries, it has been one of Ireland's most important indigenous industries. The major problem for distillers operating in Ireland has been the inability to get the right balance between the past and the future. Initially Jameson's, Power's, Bushmills, and the Cork Distillers Company failed to modernize sufficiently to meet changing circumstances in the market. When they finally began to rationalize their production facilities, they rationalized all their old distilleries out of existence, thus breaking their links with the past. Only Bushmills retained their old buildings; but the oldest of these date back only to 1890, when the distillery was rebuilt after a fire levelled the entire premises.

On 17 July 1992 Locke's pure pot still single malt Irish whiskey was launched onto the Irish and international markets. By coming to terms with the technology, marketing and finance of the modern industry, Cooley hopes to succeed where Locke's failed. Locke's provides Cooley with a distilling pedigree which goes back to the eighteenth century. This vital combination of tradition and modernity adopted by Cooley augurs well for the future of the Irish distilling industry.

NOTES

1. Companies Registration Office, Dublin, 1610/60; O'Brien and Locke to Mellor, 11 November 1963, held by Dockrell Farrell, Solicitors for Cooley.
2. For details of its restoration see J. Bailey, 'New Life at 100', *Stationary Steam Engine Research Group Bulletin*, vol. 11, no. 4.

APPENDIXES

(I would like to thank Bernard Mc Evoy of Dockrell Farrell, Solicitors, of Fitzwilliam Square, Dublin, who holds this document for Cooley Distillery.)

Schedule of Distillery in Kilbeggan
(30 November 1843)

NO. 1. DISTILLERY MILL.
Two sets of pumps, One Jack Back, two under Backs, about six hundred feet of Cooling Pipes with two Cocks. One large water wheel, pit, bull, driving, star and small wheel for sluices.

NO. 2. BREW-HOUSE.
Spent Mash. Cistern with two Cocks and Pipes about Eleven feet. Two Mash Tuns with all the machinery complete and is supposed to be in working order together with Copper Pipes for charging and discharging Mash Tuns, the pipes about two hundred feet in length by three inches. One spent Mash Pump with one shoot to the cistern to convey spent Mash. Furnace Door and some Spars to each copper.

NO. 3. ROOM OVER TUNS.
One Receiver from Pumps. One pipe attached for watering Tuns, eight feet long by two inches with Cock.
No. 1. Copper about one hundred Barrels.
No. 2. Copper about one hundred and twenty Barrels.
No. 3. Copper about ninety-eight Barrels.
No. 4. Copper about ninety-eight Barrels with Engines, lying shafts from Water Wheel to work all the ... Eight Cocks for discharging Tuns, two large troughs, to charge Wash Backs to Wash Charger.

NO. 4. BACKS.
No. 1. 178.0   inches in Height.
No. 2. 174.6   "   " Height.
No. 3. 174.8   "   " Height.
No. 4. 174.0   "   " Height.
No. 5. 170.0   "   " Height.

No. 6. 173.0 "   " Height.
No. 7. 143.0 "   " Height.
No. 8. 154.0 "   " Height.
Two Troughs for charging backs with Pipe and Cock to each Back, each about three feet long. Covers Complete.

NO. 5. RUN ROOM OR STILL HOUSE.
No. 1. Low Wines Receiver 31.5 in Height.
Charging Pipe 6 ft long by three inches.
Discharging Pipe 6 ft long with Cock.
No. 2. Low Wines Receiver 43.7 in Height.
Charging Pipe four ft by three inches.
Discharging Pipe three feet by three inches, with Cock.
No. 1. Feints receiver 32 inches High.
Charging Pipe four feet by two inches.
Discharging Pipe four feet by three inches with Cock.
No. 2. Feints receiver 42.6 inches high.
Charging Pipe 18 feet by 3 inches
Spirit receiver 34 inches High.
Discharging Pipe 60 feet by 2 inches with Cock.
No. 1. & 2. Low Wines and Feints Charger.
No. 1. 30.6 high.
No. 2. 30.0 high.
Discharging Pipes to stills 60 ft by 40 inches with two Cocks.
Pipe from Worm-Tub charging Malt Steep about 50 feet.
Wash-Charger 72.7 High. Pipe and Cock for charging Wash-Charger 8ft by 4 inches. Discharge Pipe and Cock 4ft by 5 inches. Wash-Still 8000 Imperial Gallons and valve 5 inch Cock for discharging with Head Arm, Worm and Engines perfect. No. 1. Low Wine Still and Valve 5 inch Cock for discharging with Head, Arm, Worm, and Engines perfect, all furnaces complete.

NO. 6. WORM TUB
Containing 3 worms spirit store casks.

NO. 7. SPIRIT STORE CASK 60 INCHES HIGH.
Spirit Store Cask 51.3 inches high.
Discharging pipe and cock, two inches to each.
Metal Kiln complete. Clock in gate house.

NO. 8. DISTILLERY MEAL STORES.
From No. 3 & 4 Coppers to Malt Kiln, Lofts, Pillars, Beams, and Roof new and in perfect order.

NO. 9. MALT KILN
with working floors all perfect (steep not on order) Roof over No. 1 & 2 Coppers, Lofts, and Roofs of Brew House and Distillery Mill. Also the roofs & loft of back house, Run room & floors all complete.

NO. 10. BARLEY STORE.

Beams, pillars and floor complete and in perfect order.

No. 11. LUMBER-ROOM.

Beams, loft & floor all complete.

No. 12. BONDING-STORE.

Beams, Pilars, with door and fastings all perfect.

No. 13. SPIRIT-STORE.

Floor, beams, door and window all complete.

No. 14. OFFICE.

1 large Desk, 2 Racks, 1 Grate, 1 Counter with shelves and shutters, 1 door and 2 windows, 1 small writing desk, 2 shelves in the wall, 3 high seats all in perfect order.

No. 15. MALTING-FLOORS.

No. 1. Pillars, beams and floors in perfect order.

No. 2. Do. Do. Do. in perfect order.

No. 16. STABLE.

32 feet, rack, manger and floor, machinery and utensils contained in schedule, Oat-meal-mill in possession of Messrs John and George Mullen to be delivered up with said Oat-meal-mill to John Locke esq. on the 1st November 1844. Kiln, furnace and door in perfect order. New kiln 5 spurs. no furnace.

1st Floor. 10 stone pillars, 6 new beams, 1 door, 6 windows, 1 new ben all in perfect order, Large Water Wheel. Driving, star, pit, spur and Bull Wheel, three grinding nuts, 1 speedy upright shaft with nut, 3 spindles with metal boxes, 2 pairs of grinding and 1 pair of shelling stones, 1 duster with 2 mitre wheels, 6 metal pillars with 4 metal bridges, 4 screws for rising stones.

2nd Floor. 3 Kieves for couching stones, car, hopper and damsel to each. 1 set of elevators for shelling, 1 set for meal, 1 set for raw Corn and 1 set for Dry-corn, Slow upright shaft, 1 large shoot for conveying mill Chaff to ground floor, 6 beams, 11 pillars, 1 small set of elevators for taking up cuttings, 5 windows and shutters, wooden partition and floor, one Fan, 2 ladders – all in perfect order.

3rd Floor. 6 beams, 12 wooden pillars, 4 windows and shutters, 1 sieve, 1 meal Fan, 1 pair of mitre-wheels and crank, 2 leather straps, 1 ladder, all in perfect order.

4th Floor. Frame roof, 8 pair principle rafters, 7 windows and shutters and one door, one separator, 1 shelling Fan, 4 pair of Mitre-Wheels, 2 Lying Shafts for driving elevators. Three five gallon can Imperial measure, one five gallon can Irish measure, one quart, two pints and half pint all copper.

WILLIAM CUFFE   JOHN LOCKE

APPENDIX 2

Abstract from a General Entry Book Made for Excise Purposes 1867–1901, which Describes Distillery in 1875

I, Mary Anne Locke of Kilbeggan, in the parish of Kilbeggan, and the County of Westmeath; trading under the name of John Locke and Company; do hereby revoke all former entries made by me as distiller, and do now make entry of one distillery situated in Kilbeggan, parish and county aforesaid, containing the following vessels, utensils, pipes, stores and places; that is to say;

One steam boiler, for heating worts and water used in brewing, marked steam boiler no. 1. One brewhouse, marked brewhouse no. 1. Three brewing tanks for holding worts and water, marked brewing tank no. 1, brewing tank no. 2, brewing tank no. 3. Each brewing tank has a discharge pipe with cock, which are connected with a main pipe, which conveys the worts and water to two branch pipes (on which are two cocks) and thence to mash tuns. A small pipe with cock branches from* the main pipe, and is used when the brewing tanks are cleansing. A pipe runs from one of above mentioned branch pipes to the cooling pipes; from it there is a short pipe to no. 1 underback. Each pipe has a cock on it.

The brewing tanks are connected with the steam boiler by one main and three branch pipes on which are three cocks. Two mash tuns, marked mash tun no. 1 and mash tun no. 2 for mashing. Both are connected with the brewing tanks as already described. They have two discharge pipes each with cocks, leading into no. 1 underback, and two pipes with cocks connect them with the cooling pipes, they have likewise a waste pipe each with cocks, used in cleansing them.

One malt mill room for storing malt in which is a pair of millstones for grinding malt, marked malt mill room no. 1. Two underbacks marked underback no. 1 and underback no. 2. No. 1 receives the worts from the mash tons, with which it is connected as before mentioned; and discharges itself into the cooling pipes by means of two pipes, and into no. 2 underback by a plughole; No. 2 also receives the worts from the cooling pipes through two pipes on which are cocks. A pipe from the river, for supplying water, runs into no. 2 underback which has a plughole in the bottom. Two sets of cooling pipes, marked cooling pipe no. 1, cooling pipe no. 2. They are used for cooling worts, and are connected with the underbacks as already described, and have each a waste pipe and cocks.

Six sets of pumps, viz to [very faded] marked worts pump no. 1 for pumping worts and water to backs and brewing tanks; wash pump marked wash pump no. 2 for pumping fermented wash from jack back to wash charger; Spent wash pump for pumping spent wash to its several receivers, marked spent wash pumps no.3. Water pump marked water pump no. 4 is used for supplying the steam boiler with water. Water pump, marked water pump no. 5 supplies the the worm tubs water. Spirit pump, marked spirit pump, no. 6, pumps the spirits from spirit receiver to vat in spirit store, no. 5 likewise supplies water to the malt cisterns through a pipe, which crosses distillery yard and the main road from a small water receiver at the base of the pumps. One pumping receiver, marked pumping receiver for receiving water and worts from no.1 and no. 2 pumps to which it is connected by pipes. Attached to receiver is a wooden shoot to convey worts and water to brewing tank and in the shoot are three pipes with wooden plugs. A shoot also runs from the pumping receiver to nos 1, 3, 4 and 5 backs, into each of w[?] from it runs a pipe for charging stopped by a wooden plug at top; a pipe runs from last mentioned shoot across the distillery yard, and is used for charging nos 6, 7 and 8 backs. One jack back marked jack back no.1 for receiving water and fermented wash. Three pipes enter this vessel. One from no. 2 pump, one from river and one from the fermenting back. Two of the pipes have cocks; on that to no. 2 pump has a wooden plug. One water receiver situated as already described and connected with water pumps no. 5 by a pipe and also with the river with a pipe on which there is a cock. One other pipe enters this receiver from no. 4 pump which it supplies. Three spent wash tanks, marked respectively spent wash tank no. 1, spent wash tank no. 2, spent wash tank no. 3. They are used for holding spent wash. No. 1. is supplied from both wash still discharge pipes from which sieves (two) run. Nos 2 and 3 tanks are supplied from no. 1 tank [faded] pipe runs from the latter to no. 1 tank, and a shoot and pipe to no. 2 and 3 tanks. Eight fermenting wash backs, for holding and fermenting wash, marked wash back no. 1, wash back no. 2, wash back no. 3, wash back no. 4, wash back no. 5, wash back no. 6, wash back no. 7, wash back no. 8. The first five backs are charged by down pipes from the wooden shoot connected with the pumping receiver. The last three backs are charged by down pipes from a wooden shoot connected by means of a pipe and cock with the first named shoot. All the down pipes over backs are stopped with wooden plugs. Each back has a plug hole in the bottom, and a discharge pipe with cock, which enters a main pipe connected with the jack back. The main discharge pipe from nos 6, 7, and 8 backs runs for some distance through the distillery yard, and branches into the main discharge pipe from the other back before entering the jack back. There are two cocks on the two branch pipes and one cock at entrance to jack back. [faded] marked wash charger no. 1 for receiving fermented wash. The means of charging it are a short pipe with cock connected to a wooden shoot which runs direct to no. 2 pump. It has a discharge pipe with cock, and is connected with the wash stills by two branch pipes on which are cocks. Two wash stills for distilling fermented wash into low wines, each having a head and worm, marked Wash still no. 1. content of which with head is 8436 galls, and wash still no. 2, content with head 10,320 gallons. Each wash still has a manhole door, air valve, charging pipe with cock connected with discharge pipe of wash charger, and discharge pipe with cock; from the latter run sieves to no.1 spent wash tank. Two low wines stills, each having a head and worm, marked low wines still no. 3. and low wines still no. 4. for distillery low wines and feints into feints and spirits. Content of no. 3 Low wines still and head 6080 galls. No. 4. low wines still with head 6170 gallons. Both low wines stills have a manhole door, charging pipe connected with the low wines and feints charger, air valve, and discharge pipe with cock. Each low wine still [faded] attached to their lying arms for the purpose of conveying back to the still any impure liquid which may have escaped in the process of distillation. Two worm tubs for holding the four worms of stills marked worm tub no. 1 and worm tub no. 2. No. 1 holds the worms of no. 1 wash still and the two low wines stills; no. 2, the worms of no. 2 wash still. All the worms discharge themselves into the close safe. One [?] room marked [?] room no. 1. One close safe marked close safe no. 1 for receiving low wines feints and spirits from the worms which run directly into it. One low wines and feints charger, marked low wines and feints charger no. 1. It is connected with the low wines feints receivers by means of four pipes having cocks and with the low wines still, by a main pipe from which a pipe branches off to no. 2 low wines still, both pipes have cocks. Two low wines receivers marked low wines receiver no. 1 and low wines receiver no. 2. for receiving low wines from the close safe. No. 1. low wines receiver is connected with the safe by one pipe, no. 2 low wine receiver [faded] from the safe by means of two branching pipes, running into one pipe. Two feints receivers, marked feints receiver no. 1, and feints receiver no. 2, for receiving strong and weak feints from close safe, to which is connected by a main pipe, branching into two pipes before entering into bottom of close safe. All the low wines and feints receivers have a discharge pipe and cock each, for charging the low wines and feints charger into which they run. One spirit receiver marked spirit receiver no. 1, for receiving spirits from close safe, with which it is connected by a pipe having a charging cock. It has a discharge pipe, with cock, connected with no. 6 pumps, and running from there across distillery yard to vat in spirit store. One indicator marked indicator no. 1, to which are attached the charging and discharge cock of spirit receiver. One spirit store marked spirit store no. 1. One spirit vat in spirit store marked spirit vat no. 1 for receiving spirits from no. 6 pump as described. The vat has a discharge pipe and [?].

A pipe runs from the charging pipe of the worm tubs, connected with no. 5 pump, to the top of spirit vat and into a water receiver placed there to receive water from above pipe for reducing the spirits.

One Still house marked still house no. 1. for storing fuel. In it are two furnaces carefully secured. Four grain kilns, marked kiln no. 1, kiln no. 2, kiln no. 3 and kiln no. 4, for drying raw grain. Three corn stores for storing raw grain, marked corn store no. 1, corn store no. 2, corn store no. 3, Two mills for grinding raw grain, marked mill no. 1 and mill no. 2. One cooperage for making and repairing casks in, marked cooperage no. 1. Two duty free warehouses marked duty free warehouse no. 1, duty free warehouse no. 2, for storing spirits. One grain house for receiving grains from mash tuns, marked grain house no. 1. Two back houses, marked back house no. 1, backhouse no. 2; they contain the fermenting wash backs. All pipes mentioned herein are of metal, and all places, vessels, and utensils are marked with the letter L.

Witness my hand this twentieth day of October, Eighteen hundred and Seventy five.

MARY ANNE LOCKE.

APPENDIX 3

Description of Locke's Distillery in 1886 from Alfred Barnard's The Whisky Distilleries of the United Kingdom

The Brusna Distillery is said to be the oldest in Ireland, having been founded in the year 1750. It covers nearly five acres of ground, and the adjoining lands extending for half-a-mile on the river side, are also owned by John Edward and James H. Locke. Both these young men are practical distillers, and it is owing to their enterprise that the business has increased and the output been more than doubled during the last ten years. To do this they have, from time to time, made considerable additions to the old work adding new machinery and modern appliances, still retaining, where practicable, the ancient ones, so as not to interfere with their old-fashioned Pot Stills, Mashing Vessels, and method of drying malt. The establishment, which is entirely enclosed, has a frontage to the main road of 150 feet, and entered by an archway, the clerks and Excise offices being built therein. It stands on the banks of the river from which it derives its name, and the water for both driving and mashing comes from that stream. There is such an abundant and continuous supply,. that at the time of our visit Messrs Locke & Co. were arranging to use it for electric light power in the premises. Having plenty of time, we first rambled through the old place with the partners, and afterwards commenced our duties by inspecting the Maltings, which are all built opposite the distillery proper. They are light and well ventilated buildings of five floors, capable of holding 10,000 barrels of corn. When we were there the yard at the back was crowded with farmers carts, laden with barley put up in home-made flax sacks of a primitive shape and nearly 6 feet in length. After inspection by the corn buyer, the barley is hoisted to the different floors and there spread out to a depth of 3 feet, from whence, as required, it is made to fall through traps on to the Malting Floors below, each of which possesses a stone Steep. The firm make all their own malt, being of an opinion that they can manufacture a finer quality than can be purchased.

We next ascended a staircase, and found ourselves on a level with the Kiln floors, both laid out with wire cloth and heated by open furnaces. On leaving the Kilns, we entered the Dry-Malt Stores, consisting of a three-storied stone building with slated roof, capable of storing 4,000 barrels.

We then proceeded to the Raw Grain Warehouses, which will hold 15,000 barrels of barley, to which is attached a Drying Corn Kiln, floored with Worchester perforated tiles, which seem to be in great favour with the Irish distillers. After having seen all that was of interest on this side of the way, we resumed the path from which we had deviated when we left the Distillery and entered the Mill building, a solid looking structure, containing six pairs of Mill Stones and a powerful set of Malt Rollers. Following our guide, we came to the Grist Room, a lofty chamber, 130 feet long, to which the grist is delivered by elevators. Previous to reaching the Mash House, we inspected the Brewing Tanks, which are each fitted with attemperating coils, and placed at an elevation to command the Mash Tun. In the Brewing House we observed two Mash Tuns, each with a capacity of 12,000 gallons, fitted with a double action stirring gear; the two Underbacks of timber, which hold 5,000 gallons each, are placed on the paved floor of the house, and were made on the premises. Pursuing our investigations, we next visited the Tun Room, a large apartment, containing eight Washbacks, each holding from 10,000 to 14,000 gallons, also constructed by Messrs Lockes workmen. After inspecting the Coolers, we crossed over to the Still House, a venerable building, whose outward appearance is altogether different from those we have recently visited. The first object which arrested our attention was the Wash Charger, a cast-iron vessel, placed on a gallery, holding 17,000 gallons; next the four old Pot Stills (by Miller & Co., Dublin), comprising a Wash Still, holding 10,320 gallons and 8,436 gallons; a spirit Still, 6,170 gallons, and another 6,080 gallons. In these Stills are the revolving chains; we looked inside one that had served them for years, which was as bright as a copper kettle. We have had frequent occasion to remark in the course of our lengthened tour that certain fads or customs were in use at some of the distilleries, perhaps not very important in themselves, yet they give a character to the Whisky. Here, for instance, the same method of distillation is adopted that was used by the founders of the Distillery.

Proceeding up a few steps, we came to the Can-pit Room, situated at the rear of the Still House, which contains, besides the Safe, a Low-wines and Feints Charger, also a Feints and Spirit Receiver, holding respectively 8,000 and 4,000 gallons. Adjacent is the Spirit Store, containing the usual Spirit Vat and Casking apparatus; also a duty-paid Spirit Store, which usually contains from 25 to 30 puncheons of spirits of various ages to suit the requirements of local customers.

Passing through the quadrangle, we reached the two larger Bonded stores, excellent buildings, well ventilated, which contained at the time of our visit over 2,000 casks of whisky. A short distance from these ware-houses there is a large detached building, six stories high, which, until recently, was used for making 'patent oatmeal', but the increasing demand for their 'make' led Messrs Locke and Co. to abandon that business, and it is now used for corn stores. Returning by another way, we passed the spent wash tanks, one of them, a metal vessel, holding 14,000 gallons, erected by Ross and Walpole of Dublin; also two new worm tubs, by Strong and Sons of Dublin; one of them is on a high stone arch-way, the other is covers the roof of the still house. Here we also saw the boiler house, containing a steam boiler, 32 feet long by 8 diameter, a carpenters shop, smithy, and cask shed. In the yard there is stabling for ten horses, a cart shed, and several cattle byres.

Seventy men are employed on the premises, the aged and infirm always being pensioned off or assisted. The make is 'Old Pot Still', and principally sold in Dublin, England, and the Colonies. It is both a self and blending whisky, and the annual output (1885–6) was 157,200 gallons. The plant is, however, capable of making over 200,000 gallons.

APPENDIX 4

Growth of Locke's Distillery from 1837 to 1913

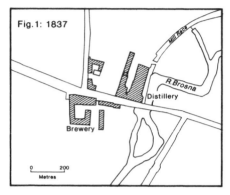

Fig.1: 1837

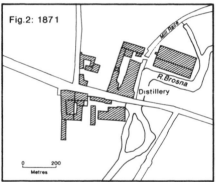

Fig.2: 1871

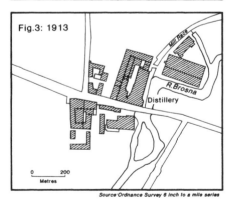

Fig.3: 1913

Source:Ordnance Survey 6 inch to a mile series

APPENDIXES

APPENDIX 5

John Locke & Co. Balance Sheet, Year Ending 30 June 1895

LIABILITIES			ASSETS		
2500 Debenture bonds of £10:	£25,000		Whiskey:	£27094 16s 6d	
4000 Ordinary shares of £10:	£40,000		Casks:	£2086 18s 0d	
			Horses, Vehicles, Saddlery:		
Sundry Creditors viz:				£256 0s 0d	
Hibernian Bank: £4694 12s 5d			Malt:	£49 10s 0d	
Less payments to 30 June '95			Barley:	£52 10s 0d	
charged to building fund a/c			Oats:	£180 7s 6d	
for new warehouse etc =			Hay:	£37 10s 0d	
£257 11s 4d	£4437 1s 1d		Straw:	£3 0s 0d	
			Coal:	£90 12s 6d	
ALL OTHERS	£1242 4s 5d		Brass Copper:	£45 0s 0d	
Cheques issued uncashed	£84 5s 0d		Sundry Debtors viz:		
Net profit for year			J.E. Locke	£3941 9s 3d	
including £142 15s 0d			J.H. Locke	£1904 15s 4d	
brought forward to credit of last account					
£5846 4s 7d					
	£7803 12s 0d				
			ALL OTHERS	£4813 1s 7d	
			Cash in hands	£129 0s 5d	
			Investment for schedule		
				£6888 18s 9d	
			Premises, Plant, Goodwill		
			written down to	£30,993 12s 8d	
TOTAL	£78567 2s 6d		TOTAL	£78567 2s 6d	

121

APPENDIX 6

John Locke & Co. Balance Sheet, Year Ending 30 June 1946

CAPITAL AND LIABILITIES				
To capital paid up 4,000 ordinary shares of £10 each	£40,000			
Debentures	£25,000			
Sundry Creditors	£16,561	17s		
" for taxation	£24,420	13s		
Hibernian Bank Ltd overdraft	£20,916	1s	2d	
Investment in Dublin Distillers Ltd. Received on account to date	£2,388			
Less value standing in books	£99	10s		
Reserve for renewal of plant etc. as per last balance sheet	£511	13s	11d	
Freight Reserve account as per last balance sheet	£400			
Reserve for Depreciation and Contingencies as per last balance sheet	£2271	0s	6d	
Net Profit and Loss Account Balance to credit	£126	9s	8d	

PROPERTY AND ASSETS				
By distillery, premises, land, plant and goodwill as per last balance sheet	£33,819	1s	10d	
Stock of whiskey and feints	£16,385	12s	6d	
Do. Casks	£279	12s	0d	
Do. Bottling materials	£155	8s	6d	
Do. Corn	£157	10s	0d	
Stationary & bill stamps	£30			
Horses Harness Drays Floats and Sundries as per last balance sheet	£10			
Motor Lorry Do. Less depreciation written off	£10			
Sundry debtors Less Reserve for bad debts and discounts	£56,563	0s	11d	
Cash on hands	£1706	7s	6d	
INVESTMENTS				
Hibernian Bank 6000 shares as per last balance sheet	£1200			
Córas Iompair Éireann as per last balance sheet	£4	15s		
1966 Debentures of £10 each in John Locke and Co. held as security by Hibernian Bank	£19,660			
Land (Meniska)	£250			
House and lands Ballinagore as per last balance sheet	£2,265			

TOTAL	£132,496	8s	3d	
TOTAL	£132,496	8s	3d	